POEMS

BY

MAURICE THOMPSON

BOSTON AND NEW YORK
HOUGHTON, MIFFLIN AND COMPANY
The Riverside Press, Cambridge
1892

The Riverside Press, Cambridge, Mass., U. S. A.
Electrotyped and Printed by H. O. Houghton & Co.

TO MY WIFE

Songs of a mocking-bird
Translated carefully,
Golden note by golden word ;
Th' original melody
Imitated phrase by phrase,
As heard in dewy dawn-lit ways
Of Freedom's solitudes
Down by the sea in the springtime woods.
Read them and heed them,
As if you heard
Prophecy out of the throat of a bird.

CONTENTS.

POEMS

IN CAPTIVITY.

You ask me why
I long to fly
Out from your palace to the dreamy woods
And the summer solitudes,
Why I pine
In this cage of mine,
Why I fret,
Why I set
All manner of querulous echoes fluttering forth
From the cold North
And wandering Southward with beseeching pain
In every strain.

Ask me not,
Task me not
With such vain questions, but fling wide the door,

And hinder me no more ;
Give back my wings to me,
And the wild currents of my liberty !

I pant,
I faint ;
I die
For the trees so high
And the broad fields of luscious cane
And the grassy plain
And the red tiled villages so old and dull,
Where (through the unkempt gardens rung)
The timbre of the Creole tongue
Makes every close so beautiful.

Oh, if you please,
Give me release !
Open the gate
Of this cage of Fate
And let me mount the south wind and go
down
To Bay Saint Louis town,
Where the brown bees hum
In amber mists of pollen and perfume ;
And the roses gush abloom !

There in the oleander groves,
With drooping wings my dear mate moves
And wonders why I stay
So long, so long away,
While the spring in fervid prime
Has waxed to nesting time,
And the air once more, in pungent ecstasy,
Whirls the wasp and butterfly,
Flings the orange petals high,
And wrings a racy thrill from every tree!

My memory turns
To a place of vines and ferns
And a cabin daubed with clay,
Where many a day
And many a sweet night long,
In the old fig-tree and the scuppernong,
I made the whole world wonder at my song.

There the restless air
Flung bubbling waves of freshness to and fro,
Where
The great japonica blossoms gleamed like snow,
While from the cabin's eaves

And from the waxen leaves
The long gray moss fell down,
Trailing like a gown.

The cabin was a home
Where naught but peace and happiness could come :
The floor was earth,
Well drained and cool, with loamy odor fine,
And on its hearth
Burned cedar boughs and knots of resinous pine
That filled the place with tender, balmy heat,
When the stout housewife broiled the juicy meat
And brewed the coffee bright and clear as wine.

There was a path down to a broad bayou,
Whose waters blue
The master of the cabin loved to sail,
In breeze or gale,
And overhead
The huge arms of an ancient live-oak spread
On high
Between the roof-rib and the violet sky.

A rout
Of noisy, wild, black children, in and out,
Ran and tumbled, leaped and sang,
Till the brakes and thickets rang
With the joy
Of girl and boy,
Who feel (and yet know not) what perfect bliss
The careless way of utter freedom is.

In the dusk of eve I heard
(Sweeter than voice of any singing bird,
Or strain of flute, or breathing of hautbois)
The ditties in patois
Warbled by two voices rich and deep,
When the brood of children had been lulled to sleep,
And man and wife sat by the cabin door,
With the rose-vine drooping o'er,
And the leaf-sounds creeping in
With a rippling soft and thin.

Ho!
A banjo!
Never was other music quite so good
For the night and the solitude,

And the fragrant, fruity silence of a Southern
wood,
And the black man's humble lot,
With its curves of simple thought,
Rounded to such rich fragments of conceit
As only nature's genius may complete.

Meantime, steadily,
In the night-light vague and high,
Angles of water-fowl winnowed the purple
sky,
Clanging their trumpet-notes
As if from brazen throats,
And seeming to fan the star-dust with their
wings,
And the breeze was like a flute,
(A Pan-flute in the reeds) blown by the lips
hirsute
Of the jovial god who loves to be where the
humblest minstrel sings.

Love-music and love-song,
Half-heathen and half-Christian, racy, strong,
Vibrant with joy, flooded with humor droll,
And rich with yearnings of the human soul,

Washed round and over me
And my sweet mate, brooding silently,
On her nest in the old fig tree —
Oh !
Open the gate and let me go !

Elusive hints
And wavering tints
Of citron blooms,
And orange foliage and the soft perfumes
Of violet and acacia come to me
On some stray current, and I hear the sea
Foaming and warm,
After a storm
And a rain,
Softening down to sleep and dreams again,
With the pelicans a-wing,
And the white gulls hovering,
And the great globe caught in the balmy palms
of Spring !

I long to be once more,
On the warm Gulf-shore,
In the dark magnolia foliage hidden quite,
With the foam-capped waves in sight,

And the vessels, wing by wing,
Gleaming and wavering
On the far horizon line,
And the sun, right overhead,
Flaring red,
And flooding with flame divine
The deep blue hollow of the sky,
And gilding the vagrant gulf-caps gloriously.
Oh, the shimmer and the sheen
On the bay and the myrtle green!
Oh, the keen bouquet
From the wax-berry fruit!
Oh, wafts that stray
O'er vines all wine from top to root!
Oh, the dull red gold in the lemon-tree!
Oh, open the cage and let me go!

Free me or I die,
Give me sweet liberty,
Whose every pulse was mine so long ago,
Down by the sea.
I feel — I feel so faint, my heart beats low,
My throat is dry and harsh —
Oh, give me back my thicket by the marsh!

Let me see the herons wade
In the watery glade,
And let me see the water-fowl go by
Glimmering against the sky.

Fainter, fainter — so,
My life-stream sinks — runs low.
Oh!
Oh!
Open the cage and let me go,
Floating, dreaming, reveling, dying, down
To my mate, my queen, my love
In the fragrant, drowsy grove
Beyond the flowery closes of Bay Saint Louis
town.

TO AN ENGLISH NIGHTINGALE.

HEAR!
Hear!
Oh, will you hear?
Reed-notes clear,
(Fluted in flowery, May-drowsed solitudes,
Filtered through sun-steeped woods)
A challenge hurled
To all the singing world!

I, the mocking bird,
Am stirred
With song's wild rapture; and the prophet's mood
Grows stronger in me with each freer breath
Of balm-buds sweet as meth;
I am no singer rude;
Here, drink my melody, spiced with things as good
As made the bragget that old Chaucer brewed.

Or if Villon
You dote upon,
I have his note and more,
And Ronsard's best in store,
Caught from a gay garçon
Who sang them clear and strong,
On Bayou Teche,
With a Creole dash
In his voice and the brim of the hat he wore!

What cheer!
What cheer!
That is the cardinal grosbeak's way,
With his sooty face and his coat so red;
Too shrill, too red, too loud and gay
(Top-knotted like a jay),
Too crude for the critical eye and ear!
In a wild plum-thicket of Tennessee
He flung a challenge out to me,
And, as Marsyas, easily
Beaten and flayed alive was he.

Cheer! Cheer!
What cheer!
Oh, all the world shall be glad to hear!

And the nightingale
Shall fail
When I burst forth with my freedom-song
So rich and strong!

Oh!
Ho!
That 's a brown thrush
In the underbrush.
Conceited, self-conscious, inclined to gush,
His is a voice that will not wear;
Faulty timbre and volume weak,
He wrings from his beak
A spiral squeak
That bores like a gimlet through the air!
And the catbird, too,
With its feline mew,
Is only fit for the springe and the snare!

I like
The shrike,
Because, with a thorn for a guillotine,
He does his work so well and clean,
A critic keen —
A practical bird,

Whose common sense
Must be immense,
For, tell me, who has ever heard
Of such a thing
As a loggerhead shrike that tried to sing?
Hear! See! Oh, see!
What do you think of me?
Do I sing by rote,
Or by note?
Have I a parrot's echo-throat?
Oh no! I caught my strains
From Nature's freshest veins.

Where blows
The Cherokee rose
Amidst Floridian hills, a slave I heard
Halloo across a green tobacco field,
And sing as gleeful as a brook or bird,
The whiles a heavy hoe his hand did wield;
I mixed his tune
With the heat of June,
And sang it
And rang it
By the slow Aucilla
And the deep Sattilla

In groves of palm and pine by tropic breezes
stirred,
And all the world has heard.

Mine is the voice of Spring,
My home is the land of the new,
And every note I sing
Is fresh as the morning dew;
For I am Freedom's bird
Whom the Pilgrim Fathers heard,
In their dreams of liberty,
Calling them to the dark wild woods across the
Western sea!

Not a mere mimic I,
That is a courtly lie
To give precedence to the nightingale
Bred in a classic vale,
Shadowed by ruins old and dim.
Give me a tilt at him!
Prestige of fame?
Romance of ages in his name?

What care I!
That bird shall die

And lie
My countless list of slain among,
On the flowery field of song!

He

A match for me!
No more than a wren or a chickadee!
Mine is the voice of the young and strong,
Mine the soul of the brave and the free!

But I can pipe the oldest runes
And trill the rarest tunes
Of every tongue in which song's perfume is.
Each swell I know,
Each quaver low,
The precious rhymes and rhythmic ecstasies
Dreamed of by master-bards long dead
And buried;
And in my treasure
The lightest measure,
Rondeau, ballade, or virelay,
To music set,
Can match the vagabond troubadour's mandore
fret for fret,
And in a key more gay
My triolet!

And when night's vast and shadowy urn
Overbrims with dreams
I stir the vales of sleep with my nocturne;
Slowly, tenderly
Outflow its rippling streams
To blend with Night's still sea of mystery;
The pungent savor of the dewy buds,
The coolness and the languor of old woods,
And the slow murmur of the darkling rills
My art distills
Into a subtle philter, wild, intense,
Of tenuous melody
And slumbrous harmony,
Blown round the dusky hills,
Through fragrant fruity tropic thickets dense,
Lingering and lapsing on,
And lost before the dawn!

Higher!
Higher!
I aspire
To Freedom's fullest note;
The vigor of waxing birdhood thrills my throat;
Morn's wide horizon, rimmed with fervid fire,
Broadens my hope

And sets far limitations to the scope
Of my desire!
Cage me not!
Enrage me not!
Confine me to no purfled garden-plot:
My song must grow, as grows the plant or tree,
Out of the sun, and earth, and winds of Liberty!

Upon no vast
Dead past
I turn my eyes;
But every budding moment's blossom I forecast,
And take each day's new melodies by surprise.
I leap to meet fresh weather,
And feel through every feather
The first delicious foretaste of a change;
I test the range
Of Nature's every franchise, every tether!

Dream on, O nightingale!
Old things shall fade and fail,
And the glory of the past shall not avail

Against the Future, all-encompassing,
Whose prophet and whose poet I would be,
Whose promise and whose meaning I shall see,
Whose fires shall flame in every note I sing !

TO AN ENGLISH SKYLARK.

Oh,
How I long to go,
On a seaward-blowing breeze,
To the garden of the seas —
To brave King Arthur's land,
To that fair island Alfred made so free,
To the haunt of chivalry,
Where master-birds sang (in the days of song)
So long
And strong!
Oh let me dwell a space by Avon's tide,
Or hide
In some old grove, where still a note may linger
Of Herrick's flute,
Of Sidney's lute,
Or of some precious rondel voiced by a forgotten singer.

Hark!
Even now I hear a lark,
The lark of England's ripe and mellow story,
The lark of England's fallow fields of glory,
Springing,
Singing,
Far and high in heaven's remotest blue,
His wings still cool with dew,
His voice (of which one song-god fair and young
A lyric of immortal fervor sung)
Still firm and true,
Still rich with exultation, rising higher,
And brimming with desire,
To fill ethereal vastness with its fire;
Forgetting love and sympathy and that law
Of human harmony
And rhythmic destiny,
Which darkly through a glass the seers and prophets saw!

O bird,
Whom gods and heroes heard
Sing in the far dim twilight hours of Time,
Whose rapture stirred

Through many a new sweet rhyme
Whilst thou didst rise
Into the skies
To purify thy song in empyrean fire!
Say where
In upper air
Dost hope to find fulfillment of thy dream?
On what far peak seest thou a morning-gleam?
Why shall the stars still blind thee unaware?
Why needst thou mount to sing?
Why seek the sun's fierce-tempered glow and glare?
Why shall a soulless impulse prompt thy wing?
Why are thy meadows and thy groves bereft
Of Freedom's inspiration, and so left
To silence in mid-spring?

O lark!
I mark,
Since Shelley died, thy wings have somewhat failed.
A precious note has faded from thy hymn,
Thy lyric fire has smouldered low and dim!
Nor ever have thy cloud-wrapt strains availed
Against the will of tyrants and the dark,

Strong doors of prisons grim,
And shackles manifold,
And dungeons cold,
Wherein sweet Freedom lies
With hopeless longing in her starry eyes
And lifeless languor on her splendid wings!
I hold
This truth as gold:
The grandest life is lowliest; he who sings
To fill the highest purpose need not soar
Above the lintel of the peasant's door,
And must not hunger for the praise of kings,
Or quench his thirst at too ethereal springs.

As for me
My life is liberty,
And close to earth's bloom-scented, fragrant floor
I gather more and more
The larger elements,
The fine suggestions of Time's last events;
I strive to know
Whither all currents flow;
I sing
On branches that the newest breezes swing;

I overreach
The limit of the present, day by day;
I teach
By shrewd anticipation, and foresay
What wider life is coming,
What joys are humming,
Like Hybla's bees, around the Future's comb;
My home
Is where all wind-tides and all perfumes meet;
Cool and clean and sweet
The young leaves rustle round my sensitive feet,
Whilst my enraptured tongue
Rolls under it
Morsels of all the songs the world's best bards have sung!

Lo! Homer's strength is mine,
And Sappho's fire divine.
And old Anacreon's flask of purple wine
Stains every note
Blown from the silvery labyrinth of my charmëd throat!
And yet the past
Has nothing in it glorious as the vast

Hope that the future holds,
Of life whose flame enfolds
The final focal thought —
The meed for which the grandest souls from
Time's first dawn have wrought.

Erewhile I lived
Where Liberty pined and grieved,
Under the sunniest of all sunny skies,
In a rich-fruited, dreamy, slumbrous paradise;
Low
And slow
The tide of human sympathy did ebb and flow.
At length, one day,
I heard a bloodhound bay;
The swamps were Freedom's sanctuary then;
Year after year
I sang the slave to cheer,
And sang to fire the hearts of earnest, freeborn
men,
Until the new day broke,
With the lifting of the yoke,
And in broad floods of sudden light divine,
I saw the slave to manhood's summit rise,
His vision set on farthest destinies,
And the slave cabin like a palace shine.

Oh, what a bliss
This love of Freedom is!
And what delight
To feel, by day and night,
Its ecstasy run deeper in my blood
While life's strong tide swells toward its highest flood!
Not in the sky
Where wastes of grandeur lie,
May genius find wherewith to slake its thirst;
The rainbow is not first
On Beauty's list,
Nor is the enchantment of heaven's highest mist
The master maker's aim!
The lowliest hearth-stone flame
Is worthier of worship than the sun!
The patter of bare brown feet that dance and run
With childish grace on the roughest cabin floor,
And the poor mother's happy smile, are more
Than starry hosts
And lofty ghosts
And awful phantoms born of overwrought
And soulless travail on the heights of thought!

Come down, O Lark, to earth,
And give a new song birth —
The song of life that grants its sweets to all,
In hut and lofty hall;
Forsake the sky,
And sky-born melody;
Fill thy meadow and thy grove
With a strain of human love —
With a wide strong pulse of music for the waiting ears of men,
Who, to be born again,
And live the life of freedom that I live,
More than their lives would give;
Yea,
Would slay,
And heap vast hecatombs, and flood
The world with blood,
And jar
Heaven with the thunder,
And the wonder
And the awful weltering whirlwind of the storm of war!

Oh, ere it is too late,
Take heed, and contemplate

What tempests sleep,
That yet will wake and leap
Across thy starry fields and blot them out,
And drown thy voice in their uproarious shout!
Thou art too high;
No longing ear or eye
May follow thee, nor is thy sweetest note
Echoed by mortal throat;
But ever it goes forth with none to hear
And none to catch its cheer!
Come sit beside me now,
Here on my orange-bough;
Forsake the legendary lights,
Forget the old hereditary heights,
And we will pipe one lusty score together
Wing by wing,
In this land of spring,
While all the world comes out to feel the weather
Throb with the fire of Freedom as we sing!

BEFORE SUNRISE.

MID foliage green and gold,
And bloom-sprays manifold,
I feel
The fragrance of eternal freshness steal
Forth from the rising day,
And far away,
Like the murmuring of a stream,
Or a lute-chord in a dream,
On the horizon stirs
The rich and rapturous anthem of the Future's choristers.
How it flows
And grows!
On its notes
What triumph floats!
Before it earth is gladdened and the sea is like a rose.

The dawn
Is coming on —

Sweeter,
Fleeter,
In rhythms and rhymes and ripples flow the rays.
The high,
Blue, boundless, splendid sky
Flares like a rimpled blaze
Of sympathy divine.
A rare
Bouquet upon the air,
As if of mellow wine
Out of old flagons bursting,
Sets the whole world wildly thirsting.
The ships leap
On the fragrant breezy deep,
And the broad fields are billowy with grains.
The great mills roar ;
Earth's veins of wealth outpour,
And tireless engines pierce the hills and crash across the plains.

Hurled
Around the world,
The lightning-bolts of man's best words to man

Burn chains in two,
Turn old things new;
And, flung back from the trumpets in the van
To the dull, listless ear
Of the straggler in the rear,
Come precious notes blown on the dewy rim
Of the morning cool and dim.

Hist!
Ere the strain is whist,
A voice, out of the dawn's vague, rosy mist:
Pure as God's highest fire
The worker's golden hire;
And the home he makes with it,
And the peace he takes with it
To wife and children, are reward as fair
As soul can compass or as love can bear.

O brothers all! come near
And hear
A bird's
Melodious dreaming set to words,
And flung
The spring's new leaves and tender buds among,

For very joy of life, and hope, and love,
In a world made broad enough
For all God's creatures to be merry in,
With joyous clash and din,
And yet too small
For any greed at all!
Lo! deep and sure
Is cut this truth in heaven's book of gold:
Out of one mother in the garden old
Were born the rich and poor.

O ditcher in the mire!
O stoker by the fire,
And driver on the engine flying far,
And brakeman on the car!
O moulder, strong and grim!
O longshoreman, and open-hearted tar,
And pilot, tough and true!
O miner in the coal-shaft damp and dim!
O factory girl with eyes serenely blue,
And cheerful matron washing clothes for hire!
O all who work and suffer and aspire!
Give ear!
Look up, and hear
And make thine own

This song, out of the future blown
So keen and clear : —
O pure of heart and faithful, hand in hand,
The strong, the weak, the great and small shall stand
Upright and free in Freedom's favored land,
And know
That howso blow
The winds of chance and change,
Onward and upward every step shall go,
And farther and freer every soul shall range !

How good
This universal bond of brotherhood,
And all this wide,
Strong, equal-flowing tide
Of human love and human charity
Foaming and heat-flushed as the rosy flood of some deep tropic sea !

No ?
Not so ? —
As I swing
And sing,

I hear a myriad voices answer mine,
From the oak woods and the pine,
From the seas and from the lakes,
From the brakes,
From the cities and the shops,
From the mines and the mountain-tops,
From field and fold,
Out of hot Southern marsh and Northern prairie cold,
All murmuring: "We are poor;
How long shall we endure
This burden that we bear
And the iron chains we wear?
What is freedom but a name?
What lot have we but poverty, — but shame?
Are we not slaves and worse?
Life is to us a bitter, burning curse!"

O brothers, though you grope
For the lowest rung of hope;
O sisters, though you weep
In darkness doubly deep,
And cry
From out foul pits of deepest misery,
Or lie
Dying in poverty,

Yet see on lofty places
Broad splendors and grand dreams
Flashing from fervent eyes and godlike faces,
Whereon the favor of Heaven divinely beams,
Envy not,
Nor curse your lot;
For lo! the best of all
God's gifts on you shall fall,
And your hearts shall overbrim
With ecstatic praise to Him!

Yea,
Deny it as you may,
The dawn
Is coming on,
And the heights must feel the glow
Before the valleys low;
But the great midday
Will strike
The peaks and vales alike
And they
Who in life's hollows stay
Shall feel the heat divine,
When the strong noon sun shall shine
At the zenith clear and high
Of a just and liberal sky!

In some manger cold,
In some hovel mean and lone
That the beasts would scorn to hold,
Laughs the babe that shall be king,
Whilst on a blazing throne
Sits an abject, hopeless thing
Silent and shivering!

O poor!
God's promises are sure;
High
As the starry sky
Is your children's destiny;
And broad
And giant-waved and tempest-bearing, like the sea,
Is the flood
That shall come roaring, leaping,
Over earth and sweeping
The horses, chariots, hosts and homes, banners and citadel
Of earth's tyrants into hell!

O king! O lord! O usurer!
O rich man's heart that no heart's cry can stir!
What gold may bar the path

Of the storm-flood and the whirlwind of God's
wrath?
What ships with iron mail,
What steel-girt fortress, what hired army
strong,
Intrenched in wrong,
With bristling guns and bayonets shall avail
Against the crushing missiles of God's ven-
geance sent
Out of the raging, rent, and foaming firmament?

It is sweet, sweet, sweet,
(I hear a million voices in unison repeat)
This vengeance that is coming on the world,
When the lofty shall lie low
And the blood of kings shall flow
In rivers round the thrones in fragments
hurled;
When the rich shall writhe and groan,
Starving in deserts lone,
When the palaces shall fall
On the lords and ladies all,
And pestilence shall stalk
Where the money-lenders walk,
And all the heavenly blue shall be a bloody
pall.

Peace!
Cease!
Such thoughts as these
Send all their harshness hissing through my
song
And do my voice irreparable wrong.

Blown clear,
As glass through fire,
Let breath of love grow sweeter year by year;
Blown farther, higher,
The bugle-call of Hope still guide us on,
Until at last
The night is past,
And, rushing to the zenith from the dawn,
We see the sun pour light of life on all,
And hear a voice out of near heaven fall,
Saying to those who in the caves and lonely
hollows dwell:
"Come forth, I am thy God, and all is well!"

Ah, well! All well!
In greening grove and dell
Hear how my song of love goes ringing on!
I am the prophet true,
My words are fresh as dew,

And lo! I say that it is morning time!
No more the darkness and the hideous rime
Of tyranny
Shall compass land and sea;
But, flaming o'er the world,
God's glorious flag of peace shall be unfurled,
And God's sweet law of liberty shall make all
nations free!

TO PROVENCE.

PROVENCE, where love and rhyme
Sweetened one throb of time ;
Provence, whose voice is dead,
Whose rose-tree vanishëd ;
Provence, old broken *broc*,
Whose melodious *Langue d'oc*,
Like sweet wine spilled and gone,
Has left a fragrance ever lingering on ;
Whose nightingale finds no new song to sing,—
I, a wild bird upon the outer rim
Of a young choir, this sunrise carol fling
Across thine ashes and thy ruins dim !

Provence,
This new song in my mouth
Is of the younger South,
Bright with the dawn of Freedom's renaissance,
The South that has no care
For the sad, grim cavalier,
Dreaming of flaunting flag and crashing lance,

And all unmindful of the day and year
Whereon the world took leave of old romance.

The South whose gaze is cast
No more upon the past,
But whose bright eyes the skies of promise sweep,
Whose feet in paths of progress swiftly leap;
And whose fresh thoughts, like cheerful rivers run,
Through odorous ways to meet the morning sun!

Gone is thy troubadour,
Gone the soft clamor of thy *cour d'amour*,
Rondeau, ballade, chanson;
And the plaudits that they won
Echo no more along the sheeny Rhone.
All desolate! And why is this?
Where is that splendid thing
That leaped from thee on many-colored wing?
Thou lifeless chrysalis!

Remembered as a dream,
Thy soft song glories seem

To hover on Time's outmost purple bound;
Thy hautbois and guitar —
They touch us with the merest film of sound!

Provence,
Wafts of thy *gaie science*
Still lightly pass, whereto we do not know,
Like some frail, fine perfume,
From a paradise of bloom
Fallen to golden dust five hundred years ago!

Thou art the old, dead South,
Given over unto drouth;
Given over unto memory, unto dust,
Unto mildew, unto must,
With a false smack of chivalry in thy mouth,
Mumbling, in false pride, thy miserable crust!

My South, too, was dead,
And on her corse the ghoul of slavery fed;
But the resurrection came,
And a new life leaped, like flame,
In every breast!
Oh, it was joy to see
The slave ride down the lists of Liberty,

With shining shield and leveled lance in rest,
His swart face lifted high,
His eyes on destiny,
While Lincoln's hand erased the inscription old
Of the nation's palimpsest,
And wrote thereon, in words of fire and gold,
Freedom, from North to South, from East to West!

Ah! what was dust
Is dew!
And what was rust
Is new!
The breath of death is gone,
And life goes pouring on
In a bright flood.
No more
The cannon's roar,
And the blue sky is tinged no more with blood,
Whilst from the mountains to the shining sea,
The peace of morning evermore shall be!

Provence, turn, turn away,
From thy long yesterday,

And see how fair to-morrow's promise shines!
What is the past but death?
How fresh the Future's breath!
Awake. 'T is morn. Thy orchards and thy vines
Are rich with bloom,
The mistral throbs ecstatic with perfume,
And fans to flame thine ashes with its wings!
Lo, the Republic makes
Life out of death, and takes
Even ruin captive with the song it sings!

TO SAPPHO.

NOTE.—The italicized parts of this poem are translations of the Fragments of Sappho, and I have thought to weave them in as echoes, in the true mocking bird manner.

Up from the Caribbean
The wind comes like a pæan,
As on my fragrant orange-bough I swing,
Dreaming, and wondering,
And piping Sapphic fragments o'er and o'er.

Along the shore
The surf foams madly and the breakers roar.
Strange odors from afar,
Spice, amber, nard, and tar,
And Lesbian roses grown in Mitylene,
And violet breath, and waft of myrtle green,
Steep me in visions passionate and wild,
Of love, all undefiled,
Whereby was Sappho's bright
Rose garden of delight,
Flooded with starry splendors of old night!

A bower of June,
With morning freshness lingering after noon
Upon the petals of the passion-rose;
All round through apple boughs the cool air blows,
Shaking soft slumber down the dusky leaves,
Where still the subtle violet-weaver weaves!

Eden of Love's own choice,
Haunted of Love's own voice,
Thy ways I could not take —
Nay, not for Sappho's sake,
And leave my orange grove
And the fresh promise of the land I love!
Liberty,
Wild liberty,
Not license, give to me!
Give me the glory of what is to come —
Fill me with prophecy — the mighty hum
Of swarming years and wonders yet to be!
And still, O Sappho! still I turn and sigh
That all but these stray notes of all thy songs
should die;
That these chance fragments old,
Of things more golden than the virgin gold,
To music set beyond all melody,

Have come to me,
Of all thy treasure, blown across the sea!

Mad maid of Mitylene,
Song-slave, song-mistress, and song-queen!
Blessëd the nightingale
Whom thou didst sing
And hail
As tender messenger of Spring!
Sappho, oh thou —
Sweet-apple on the bough,
Yea, blushing on the top spray of the tree,
Whom all the apple gatherers failed to see,
Nay, saw, but could not reach, and cannot now,
Thy song perforce will fill my throat
And burn it with each golden, molten note!
Who knows thee best
Knows never peace or rest,
And yet his every thought
Is a joy from Heaven caught;
And his heart-flower open blows
Like a dark red Lesbian rose!
God-like he thrones himself, who sits by thee,
And feels the dear delirium of thy words,
And of thy laughter hears the tender chords!

The vision thrills my heart; for if I see,
In merest glimpse, thy form, my voice fails me,
My tongue is numb, with fire my blood is shot,
My ears hum, and my straining eyes see not,
My frame, bedewed with madness, quivereth
And, paler than pale grass, I look like death!

Oh, not in wanton whirls
Thy singing bevy sweet
Danced round thee on charmed feet,
Oh, blessëd girls!
Who felt thy song-breath on their shining curls
And thy fierce flame of longing in their veins!
What delicate, deep, delicious bitterness,
What stress
Of overmastering, sad ecstasy within
Each quivering heart! What glorious din
Of girlish voices and love-smitten lyres!
What incense from what all-consuming fires!

O Sappho, didst thou sing
This haunting, saddening thing?—
Ever shalt thou lie dead,
No more rememberëd,
Since no Pierian roses blew for thee,

Unnoticed mid the shadows dim and dread,
Alone in the hereafter shalt thou be!
Didst thou mean me?

But what care I?
I shall not die,
For Liberty lends to me her deathless wing;
My land is the eternal home of spring,
Beyond all clouds my purple dome of sky,
The nations hunger for the songs I sing
Making the New World's groves with Freedom's transports ring!
Naught have I for the tomb,
Blooming, as centuries bloom,
Fairer with each new day,
No petal of my song-flower shall decay!
Not so with thine,
Veined like the lily's, as the rose's fine;
Plucked by the vulgar hand of comedy,
They scent the desert dust and sweeten all the sea!

Pressed thin between the pages
Of the torn book of ages,
Suggestive of what fragrant thoughts it is

To find a bloom like this :
Last night I spoke with Venus in my dream!
Ah, in what bower of bliss,
By what Pan-haunted stream,
Didst thou the lips of Aphrodite kiss?

What *bitter-sweet*
Wild love shook thee from head to feet,
And tore thy breast,
Like a wind that rends the oak-tree on the moun-
tain's crest?
What garland didst thou wear?
And who was Althis fair,
Loved once, loved madly, loved so long ago?
And oh!
For whom didst thou lie lonesome when the moon
had set,
And the Pleiades were down?
What purple gown
Didst thou quit wearing when thy love came
not?
And (O delicate thought!)
For thy lost girlhood crying all in vain,
What strange, wild joys were caught
And tangled in thy pain?

Far in the night,
When the moon sails high and white,
In the rich, dark firmament,
And the sea-wind is spent,
And the magnolia's heavy flowers are hung,
Like ghastly death-bells waiting to be rung,
I yearn
In a low, many-toned, deep, sweet nocturne,
To guess,
And so express,
The lost notes that, once stricken from thy lyre,
Touched all the world with fiery tenderness,
And filled the air with veins of tender fire;
But of my longing *cometh unto me*
Never the bubbling honey, nor the honey-bee!

Nay,
Never tongue may say
What founts of inspiration and delight
Forsook the day, what stars shrank from the night,
When all thy songs,
Torn into shreds and smirched with foulest wrongs,

Were scattered,
Battered,
Bruised, and so left to lie
In places lone and high,
Dark petals of a hyacinth, odorous still,
Crushed by rude feet on many a windy hill!

PROEM.

THOUGH I am poor, and cannot buy
The rare, time-mellowed things of Art,
God keeps an open gallery
Of glories for the poor in heart,
Whose walls are hung with grander show
Of color than old Titian knew,
With outlines Michael Angelo
Wronged in the best cartoons he drew!

All this is mine to have and hold:
Nor fire may burn, nor years may soil,
With ruthless trace of gathering mould,
These wonders of the Master's toil;
Nor can some restless child of Fate,
Some darkly gifted Corsican,
By red successes decorate
His Louvre from my Vatican!

AN EARLY BLUEBIRD.

Leap to the highest height of spring,
  And trill thy sweetest note,
Bird of the heavenly plumes and twinkling
    wing
  And silver-tonëd throat!

Sing, while the maple's deepest root
  Thrills with a pulse of fire
That lights its buds. Blow, blow thy tender
    flute,
  Thy reed of rich desire!

Breathe in thy syrinx Freedom's breath,
  Quaver the fresh and true,
Dispel this lingering wintry mist of death
  And charm the world anew!

Thou first sky-dipped spring-bud of song,
  Whose heavenly ecstasy

Foretells the May while yet March winds are strong,
Fresh faith appears with thee!

How sweet, how magically rich,
Through filmy splendor blown,
Thy hopeful voice set to the promise-pitch
Of melody yet unknown!

O land of mine (where hope can grow
And send a deeper root
With every spring), hear, heed the free bird blow
Hope's charmëd flute!

Ah! who will hear, and who will care,
And who will heed thy song,
As prophecy, as hope, as promise rare,
Budding to bloom ere long?

From swelling bulbs and sprouting seed,
Sweet sap and fragrant dew,
And human hearts, grown doubly warm at need,
Leaps answer strong and true:

We see, we hear (thou liberty-loving thing,
  That down spring winds doth float),
The promise of thine empyrean wing,
  The hope that floods thy throat!

A PRELUDE.

SPIRIT that moves the sap in spring,
When lusty male birds fight and sing,
Inform my words, and make my lines
As sweet as flowers, as strong as vines.

Let mine be the freshening power
Of rain on grass, of dew on flower;
The fertilizing song be mine,
Nut-flavored, racy, keen as wine.

Let some procreant truth exhale
From me, before my forces fail;
Or ere the ecstatic impulse go,
Let all my buds to blossoms blow.

If quick, sound seed be wanting where
The virgin soil feels sun and air,
And longs to fill a higher state,
There let my meanings germinate.

Let not my strength be spilled for naught,
But, in some fresher vessel caught,
Be blended into sweeter forms,
And fraught with purer aims and charms.

Let bloom-dust of my life be blown
To quicken hearts that flower alone;
Around my knees let scions rise
With heavenward-pointed destinies.

And when I fall, like some old tree,
And subtile change makes mould of me,
There let earth show a fertile line
Whence perfect wild-flowers leap and shine.

THE ARCHER.

THE joy is great of him who strays
In shady woods on summer days,
With eyes alert and muscles steady,
His longbow strung, his arrows ready.

At morn he hears the woodthrush sing,
He sees the wild rose blossoming,
And on his senses, soft and low,
He feels the brook-song ebb and flow.

Life is a charm, and all is good
To him who lives like Robin Hood,
Hearing ever, far and thin,
Hints of the tunes of Gamelyn.

His greatest grief, his sharpest pain,
Is (when the days are dark with rain)
That for a season he must lie
Inert, while deer go bounding by ;

Lounge in his lodge, and long and long
For Allen a Dale's delightful song,
Or smack his lips at thought of one
Drink from the Friar's demijohn.

But when the sky is clear again,
He sloughs his grief, forgets his pain,
Hearing on gusts of charming weather
The low laugh of his arrow feather!

THE DEATH OF THE WHITE HERON.

(CYPRESS LAKE, FLORIDA.)

I PULLED my boat with even sweep
Across light shoals and eddies deep,

Tracking the currents of the lake
From lettuce raft to weedy brake.

Across a pool death-still and dim
I saw a monster reptile swim,

And caught, far off and quickly gone,
The delicate outlines of a fawn.

Above the marshy islands flew
The green teal and the swift curlew ;

The rail and dunlin drew the hem
Of lily-bonnets over them ;

I saw the tufted wood-duck pass
Between the wisps of water-grass.

All round the gunwales and across
I draped my boat with Spanish moss,

And, lightly drawn from head to knee,
I hung gay air-plants over me ;

Then, lurking like a savage thing
Crouching for a treacherous spring,

I stood in motionless suspense
Among the rushes green and dense.

I kept my bow half-drawn, a shaft
Set straight across the velvet haft.

Alert and vigilant, I stood
Scanning the lake, the sky, the wood.

I heard a murmur soft and sad
From water-weed to lily-pad,

And from the frondous pine did ring
The hammer of the golden-wing.

On old drift-logs the bittern stood
Dreaming above the silent flood ;

The water-turkey eyed my boat,
The hideous snake-bird coiled its throat,

And birds whose plumage shone like flame, —
Wild things grown suddenly, strangely tame, —

Lit near me ; but I heeded not :
They could not tempt me to a shot.

Grown tired at length, I bent the oars
By grassy brinks and shady shores,

Through labyrinths and mysteries
Mid dusky cypress stems and knees,

Until I reached a spot I knew,
Over which each day the herons flew.

I heard a whisper sweet and keen
Flow through the fringe of rushes green,

The water saying some light thing,
The rushes gayly answering.

The wind drew faintly from the south,
Like breath blown from a sleeper's mouth,

And down its current sailing low
Came a lone heron white as snow.

He cleft with grandly spreading wing
The hazy sunshine of the spring;

Through graceful curves he swept above
The gloomy moss-hung cypress grove;

Then gliding down a long incline,
He flashed his golden eyes on mine.

Half-turned he poised himself in air,
The prize was great, the mark was fair!

I raised my bow, and steadily drew
The silken string until I knew

My trusty arrow's barbëd point
Lay on my left forefinger joint, —

Until I felt the feather seek
My ear, swift-drawn across my cheek:

Then from my fingers leapt the string
With sharp recoil and deadly ring,

Closed by a sibilant sound so shrill,
It made the very water thrill, —

Like twenty serpents bound together,
Hissed the flying arrow's feather!

A thud, a puff, a feathery ring,
A quick collapse, a quivering,

A whirl, a headlong downward dash,
A heavy fall, a sullen plash, —

And like white foam, or giant flake
Of snow, he lay upon the lake.

And of his death the rail was glad,
Strutting upon a lily-pad;

The jaunty wood-duck smiled and bowed;
The belted kingfisher laughed aloud,

Making the solemn bittern stir
Like a half-wakened slumberer;

And rasping notes of joy were heard
From gallinule and crying-bird,

The while with trebled noise did ring
The hammer of the golden-wing!

A FLIGHT SHOT.

We were twin brothers, tall and hale,
Glad wanderers over hill and dale.

We stood within the twilight shade
Of pines that rimmed a Southern glade.

He said: "Let 's settle, if we can,
Which of us is the stronger man.

"We 'll try a flight shot, high and good,
Across the green glade toward the wood."

And so we bent in sheer delight
Our old yew bows with all our might.

Our long keen shafts, drawn to the head,
Were poised a moment ere they sped.

As we leaned back a breath of air
Mingled the brown locks of our hair.

We loosed. As one our bow-cords rang,
As one away our arrows sprang.

Away they sprang; the wind of June
Thrilled to their softly whistled tune.

We watched their flight, and saw them strike
Deep in the ground slantwise alike,

So far away that they might pass
For two thin straws of broom-sedge grass!

Then arm in arm we doubting went
To find whose shaft was farthest sent,

Each fearing in his loving heart
That brother's shaft had fallen short.

But who could tell by such a plan
Which of us was the stronger man?

There at the margin of the wood,
Side by side our arrows stood,

Their red cock-feathers wing and wing,
Their amber nocks still quivering,

Their points deep-planted where they fell
An inch apart and parallel!

We clasped each other's hands; said he,
"Twin champions of the world are we!"

THE FAWN.

I LAY close down beside the river,
My bow well strung, well filled my quiver.

The god that dwells among the reeds
Sang sweetly from their tangled bredes ;

The soft-tongued water murmured low,
Swinging the flag-leaves to and fro.

Beyond the river, fold on fold,
The hills gleamed through a film of gold ;

The feathery osiers waved and shone
Like silver threads in tangles blown.

A bird, fire-winged, with ruby throat,
Down the slow, drowsy wind did float,

And drift and flit and stay along,
A very focal flame of song.

A white sand-isle amid the stream
Lay sleeping by its shoals of bream ;

In lilied pools, alert and calm,
Great bass through lucent circles swam ;

And farther, by a rushy brink,
A shadowy fawn stole down to drink,

Where tall, thin birds unbalanced stood
In sandy shallows of the flood.

And what did I beside the river,
With bow well-strung and well-filled quiver ?

I lay quite still with half-closed eyes,
Lapped in a dream of Paradise,

Until I heard a bow-cord ring,
And from the reeds an arrow sing.

I knew not of my brother's luck,
If well or ill his shaft had struck ;

But something in his merry shout
Put my sweet summer dream to rout,

And up I sprang, with bow half-drawn,
And keen desire to slay the fawn.

But where was it? Gone like my dream.
I only heard the fish-hawk scream,

And the strong stripëd bass leap up
Beside the lily's floating cup;

I only felt the cool wind go
Across my face with steady flow;

I only saw those thin birds stand
Unbalanced on the river sand,

Low peering at some dappled thing
In the green rushes quivering.

THE BLUE HERON.

WHERE water-grass grows overgreen
  On damp cool flats by gentle streams,
Still as a ghost and sad of mien,
  With half-closed eyes the heron dreams.

Above him in the sycamore
  The flicker beats a dull tattoo;
Through pawpaw groves the soft airs pour
  Gold dust of blooms and fragrance new.

And from the thorn it loves so well,
  The oriole flings out its strong,
Sharp lay, wrought in the crucible
  Of its flame-circled soul of song.

The heron nods. The charming runes
  Of Nature's music thrill his dreams;
The joys of many Mays and Junes
  Wash past him like cool summer streams.

What tranquil life, what joyful rest,
  To feel the touch of fragrant grass,
And doze like him, while tenderest
  Dream-waves across my sleep would pass!

THE BLUEBIRD.

WHEN ice is thawed and snow is gone,
  And racy sweetness floods the trees ;
When snow-birds from the hedge have flown,
  And on the hive-porch swarm the bees, —
Drifting down the first warm wind
  That thrills the earliest days of spring,
The bluebird seeks our maple groves,
  And charms them into tasseling.

He sits among the delicate sprays,
  With mists of splendor round him drawn,
And through the spring's prophetic veil
  Sees summer's rich fulfillment dawn :
He sings, and his is nature's voice, —
  A gush of melody sincere
From that great fount of harmony
  Which thaws and runs when spring is here.

Short is his song, but strangely sweet
  To ears aweary of the low,

Dull tramp of Winter's sullen feet,
  Sandaled in ice and muffed in snow:
Short is his song, but through it runs
  A hint of dithyrambs yet to be, —
A sweet suggestiveness that has
  The influence of prophecy.

From childhood I have nursed a faith
  In bluebird's songs and winds of spring:
They tell me after frost and death
  There comes a time of blossoming;
And after snow and cutting sleet,
  The cold, stern mood of Nature yields
To tender warmth, when bare pink feet
  Of children press her greening fields.

Sing strong and clear, O bluebird dear!
  While all the land with splendor fills,
While maples gladden in the vales
  And plum-trees blossom on the hills:
Float down the wind on shining wings,
  And do thy will by grove and stream,
While through my life spring's freshness runs
  Like music through a poet's dream.

THE WABASH.

THERE is a river singing in between
Bright fringes of pawpaw and sycamore,
That stir to fragrant winds on either shore,
Where tall blue herons stretch lithe necks, and
lean
Over clear currents flowing cool and thin
Through the clean furrows of the pebbly floor.

My own glad river. Though unclassic, still
Haunted of merry gods whose pipings fill
With music all thy golden willow-brakes!
Above thee halcyon lifts his regal crest;
The tulip-tree flings thee its flower-flakes,
The tall flag over thee its lances shakes:
With every charm of beauty thou art blest,
O happiest river of the happy West!

OKECHOBEE.

THY shadowy margin, O still, tropic lake,
Is like a thought that hovers in the brain
Beyond the reach of phrase to make it plain,
Divinely sweet for its dim mystery's sake.
The real and the ideal, matched so well
In yonder palm-trees and their ghosts below,
Have but a doubtful line between to tell
That from a common root they do not grow!

The delicate shifting shades that cloud the sheen
Of water too harmonious to flow,
Flit over tufts of flags and willows green,
Which feel not even the faintest summer swell.

. . . .

O Lake, thy beauty inexpressible is
Except by some song-wrought antholysis!

DROPPING CORN.

PRETTY Phœbe Lane and I,
In the soft May weather,
Barefoot down the furrows went
Dropping corn together.

Side by side across the field
Back and forth we hurried;
All the golden grains we dropped
Soon the ploughshare buried.

Bluebirds on the hedges sat,
Chirping low and billing;
"Why," thought I, "not follow suit,
If the maid is willing?"

So I whispered, "Phœbe, dear,
Kiss me" — "Keep on dropping!"
Called her father from the plough;
"There 's no time for stopping!"

The cord was loosed, — the moment sped ;
  The golden charm was broken !
Nevermore between us two
  Word of love was spoken.

What a little slip, sometimes,
  All our hope releases !
How the merest breath of chance
  Breaks our joy in pieces !

Sorrow's cup, though often drained,
  Never lacks for filling ;
And we can't get Fortune's kiss
  When the maid is willing !

THE MORNING HILLS.

I.

He sits among the morning hills,
  His face is bright and strong;
He scans far heights, but scarcely notes
  The herdsman's idle song.

He cannot brook this peaceful life
  While battle's trumpet calls;
He sees a crown for him who wins,
  A tear for him who falls.

The flowery glens and shady slopes
  Are hateful to his eyes;
Beyond the heights, beyond the storms,
  The land of promise lies.

II.

He is so old and sits so still,
  With face so weak and mild,

We know that he remembers naught
  Save when he was a child.

His fight is fought, his fame is won,
  Life's highest peak is past;
The laurel crown, the triumph-arch,
  Are worthless at the last.

The frost of age destroys the bay, —
  The loud applause of men
Falls feebly on the palsied ears
  Of threescore years and ten.

He does not hear the voice that bears
  His name around the world;
He has no thought of great deeds done
  Where battle-tempests whirled;

But evermore he is looking back,
  Whilst memory fills and thrills
With echoes of the herdsman's song
  Among the morning hills.

AT THE WINDOW.

I HEARD the woodpecker pecking,
  The bluebird tenderly sing;
I turned and looked out of my window,
  And lo, it was spring!

A breath from tropical borders,
  Just a ripple, flowed into my room,
And washed my face clean of its sadness,
  Blew my heart into bloom.

The loves I have kept for a lifetime,
  Sweet buds I have shielded from snow,
Break forth into full leaf and tassel
  When spring winds do blow.

For the sap of my life goes upward,
  Obeying the same sweet law
That waters the heart of the maple
  After a thaw.

I forget my old age and grow youthful,
  Bathing in wind-tides of spring,
When I hear the woodpecker pecking,
  The first bluebird sing.

NOVEMBER.

A HINT of slumber in the wind,
  A dreamful stir of blades and stalks,
As tenderly the twilight flows
  Down all my garden walks.

My robes of work are thrown aside,
  The odor of the grass is sweet;
The pleasure of a day well spent
  Bathes me from head to feet.

Calmly I wait the dreary change, —
  The season cutting sharp and sheer
Through the wan bowers of death that fringe
  The border of the year.

And while I muse, the fated earth
  Into a colder current dips, —
Feels winter's scourge, with summer's kiss
  Still warm upon her lips.

BETWEEN THE POPPY AND THE ROSE.

How tired! Eight hours of racking work,
  With sharp vexations shot between!
Scant wages and few kindly words, —
  How gloomy the whole day has been!
But here is home. The garden shines,
  And over it the soft air flows;
A mist of chastened glory hangs
  Between the poppy and the rose.

The poppy red as ruby is,
  The rose pale pink, fullblown, and set
Amid the dark rich leaves that form
  The strong vine's royal coronet;
And half-way o'er from this to that,
  In a charmed focus of repose,
Two rare young faces, lit with love,
  Between the poppy and the rose.

Sweet little Jessie, two years old,
  Dear little Mamma, twenty-four,

Together in the garden walk
  While evening sun-streams round them pour.
List! Mamma murmurs baby-talk!
  Hush! Jessie's talk to laughter glows!
They both look heavenly sweet to me,
  Between the poppy and the rose.

Two flakes of sunshine in deep shade,
  Two diamonds set in rougher stone,
Two songs with harp accompaniment
  Across a houseless desert blown, —
No, nothing like this vision is;
  How deep its innocent influence goes,
Sweeter than song or power or fame,
  Between the poppy and the rose!

Between the poppy and the rose,
  A bud and blossom shining fair,
A childlike mother and a child,
  Whose own my very heart-throbs are!
Oh, life is sweet, they make it so;
  Its work is lighter than repose:
Come anything, so they bloom on
  Between the poppy and the rose.

SOLACE.

THOU art the last rose of the year,
  By gusty breezes rudely fanned:
The dying Summer holds thee fast
  In the hot hollow of her hand.

Thy face pales, as if looking back
  Into the splendor of thy past
Had thrilled thee strangely, knowing that
  This one long look must be the last.

Thine essence, that was heavenly sweet,
  Has flown upon the tricksy air:
Fate's hand is on thee ; drop thy leaves,
  And go among the things that were.

Be must and mould, be trampled dust,
  Be nothing that is fair to see :
One day, at least, of glorious life
  Was thine of all eternity.

Be this a comfort : crown and lyre
  And regal purple last not long ;
Kings fall like leaves, but thy perfume
  Strays through the years like royal song.

HO, FOR THE KANKAKEE!

Ho, for the marshes, green with Spring,
  Where the bitterns croak and the plovers
    pipe,
Where the gaunt old heron spreads his wing,
  Above the haunt of rail and snipe ;
For my gun is clean and my rod 's in trim,
  And the old, wild longing is roused in me ;
Ho, for the bass-pools cool and dim !
  Ho, for the swales of the Kankakee!

Is there other joy like the joy of a man
  Free for a season with rod and gun,
With the sun to tan and the winds to fan,
  And the waters to lull, and never a one
Of the cares of life to follow him,
  Or to shadow his mind while he wanders free ?
Ho, for the currents slow and dim !
  Ho, for the fens of the Kankakee !

A hut by the river, a light canoe,
  My rod and my gun, and a sennight fair —
A wind from the South, and the wildfowl due
  Be mine. All 's well. Comes never a care.
A strain of the savage fires my blood,
  And the zest of freedom is keen in me;
Ho, for the marsh and the lilied flood!
  Ho, for the sloughs of the Kankakee!

Give me to stand where the swift currents rush,
  With my rod all astrain and a bass coming in,
Or give me the marsh, with the brown snipe aflush,
  And my gun's sudden flashes and resonant din;
For I am tired of the desk, and tired of the town,
  And I long to be out, and I long to be free:
Ho, for the marsh, with the birds whirling down!
  Ho, for the pools of the Kankakee!

ATALANTA.

WHEN Spring grows old, and sleepy winds
  Set from the south with odors sweet,
I see my love, in green, cool groves,
  Speed down dusk aisles on shining feet.

She throws a kiss and bids me run,
  In whispers sweet as roses' breath;
I know I cannot win the race,
  And at the end I know is death.

But joyfully I bare my limbs,
  Anoint me with the tropic breeze,
And feel through every sinew thrill
  The vigor of Hippomenes.

O race of love! we all have run
  Thy happy course through groves of spring,
And cared not, when at last we lost,
  For life or death, or anything!

THE SENTINEL.

WHAT of this Hour that passes
 With a shimmer of gold and blue?
O Love, through your crystal glasses
 What seems this hour to you?
 I see the gold and blue
Of the beautiful thing that passes
On the wind through the summer grasses,
 But it is nothing new!

Halt! sweet Hour, I stand on guard;
 You cannot pass this way!
My heart (my master) bids me ward
 His outer court to-day;
 Stop where you are, and stay.
Your face would witch full many a guard,
But I am old and stern and hard;
 Beware, I say!

What of this bright Hour, standing
 Just out before the gate,

A passage of right demanding
    Because it groweth late ?
    O Love, must I ope the gate ?
See, see the bright thing standing,
Sharp, scintillant, commanding !
    Is it a fate ?

AT NIGHT.

THE moon hangs in a silver mist,
  The stars are dull and thin ;
Sleep, bending low, spreads loving arms
  To fold the whole world in.
The air is like a spell ; the hills
  Waver, now seen, now lost ;
The pallid river wanders by,
  A vast unquiet ghost.

A hornëd owl on silent wings,
  From out a cavernous place,
Speeds, like a bolt of darkness hurled
  Athwart the shining space
Above the vale from wood to wood,
  And leaves no trace behind, —
Like some dark fancy flung across
  A pure and peaceful mind !

IN EXILE.

I.

THE singing streams, and the deep, dark wood
Beloved of old by Robin Hood,

Lift me a voice, kiss me a hand,
To call me from this younger land.

What time by dull Floridian lakes,
What time by rivers fringed with brakes,

I blow the reed, and draw the bow,
And see my arrows hurtling go

Well sent to deer or wary hare,
Or wildfowl whistling down the air;

What time I lie in shady spots
On beds of wild forget-me-nots,

That fringe the fen lands insincere
And boggy marges of the mere,

Whereon I see the heron stand,
Knee-deep in sable slush of sand, —

I think how sweet if friends should come
And tell me England calls me home.

II.

I keep good heart, and bide my time,
And blow the bubbles of my rhyme ;

I wait and watch, for soon I know
In Sherwood merry horns shall blow,

And blow and blow, and folk shall come
To tell me England calls me home.

Mother of archers, then I go
Wind-blown to you with bended bow,

To stand close up by you and ask
That it be my appointed task

To sing in leal and loyal lays
Your matchless bowmen's meed of praise ;

And that unchallenged I may go
Through your green woods with bended bow, —

Your woods where bowered and hidden stood
Of old the home of Robin Hood.

Ah, this were sweet, and it will come
When merry England calls me home!

III.

Perchance, long hence, it may befall,
Or soon, mayhap, or not at all,

That all my songs nowhither sent,
And all my shafts at random spent,

Will find their way to those who love
The simple force and truth thereof;

Wherefore my name shall then be rung
Across the land from tongue to tongue,

Till some who hear shall haste to come
With news that England calls me home.

I walk where spiced winds raff the blades
Of sedge-grass on the summer glades ;

Through purfled blades that fringe the mere
I watch the timid tawny deer

Set its quick feet and quake and spring,
As if it heard some deadly thing,

When but a brown snipe flutters by
With rustling wing and piping cry ;

I stand in some dim place at dawn,
And see across a forest lawn

The tall wild turkeys swiftly pass
Light-footed through the dewy grass ;

I shout, and wind my horn, and go
The whole morn through with bended bow,

Then on my rest I feel at noon
Sown pulvil of the blooms of June ;

I live and keep no count of time,
I blow the bubbles of my rhyme :

These are my joys till friends shall come
And tell me England calls me home.

IV.

The self-yew bow was England's boast;
She leaned upon her archer host, —

It was her very life-support
At Crecy and at Agincourt,

At Flodden and at Halidon Hill,
And fields of glory redder still!

O bows that rang at Solway Moss!
O yeomanry of Neville's cross!

These were your victories, for by you
Breastplate and shield were cloven through;

And mailëd knights at every joint
Sore wounded by an arrow point,

Drew rein, turned pale, reeled in the sell,
And, bristled with arrows, gasped and fell!

O barbëd points that scratched the name
Of England on the walls of fame!

O music of the ringing cords
Set to grand song of deeds, not words!

O yeomen! for your memory's sake,
These bubbles of my rhyme I make, —

Not rhymes of conquest stern and sad,
Or hoarse-voiced like the Iliad,

But soft and dreamful as the sigh
Of this sweet wind that washes by, —

The while I wait for friends to come
And tell me England calls me home.

V.

I wait and wait; it would be sweet
To feel the sea beneath my feet,

And hear the breeze sing in the shrouds
Betwixt me and the white-winged clouds, —

To feel and know my heart should soon
Have its desire, its one sweet boon,

To look out on the foam-sprent waste
Through which my vessel's keel would haste,

Till on the far horizon dim
A low white line would shine and swim;

The low white line, the gleaming strand,
The pale cliffs of the Mother-land!

O God! the very thought is bliss,
The burden of my song it is,

Till over sea song-blown shall come
The news that England calls me home!

VI.

Ah, call me, England, some sweet day
When these brown locks are silver gray,

And these brown arms are shrunken small,
Unfit for deeds of strength at all;

When the swift deer shall pass me by,
Whilst all unstrung my bow shall lie,

And birds shall taunt me with the time
I wasted making foolish rhyme,

And wasted blowing in a reed
The runes of praise, the yeoman's meed,

And wasted dreaming foolish dreams
Of English woods and English streams,

Of grassy glade and queachy fen
Beloved of old by archer men,

And of the friends who would not come
To tell me England called me home.

VII.

Such words are sad : blow them away
And lose them in the leaves of May,

O wind ! and leave them there to rot,
Like random arrows lost when shot ;

And here, these better thoughts, take these
And blow them far across the seas,

To that old land and that old wood
Which hold the dust of Robin Hood!

Say this, low-speaking in my place:
"The last of all the archer race

"Sends this his sheaf of rhymes to those
Whose fathers bent the self-yew bows,

"And made the cloth-yard arrows ring
For merry England and her king,

"Wherever Lion Richard set
His fortune's stormy banneret!"

Say this, and then, oh, haste to come
And tell me England calls me home!

BEFORE DAWN.

A KEEN, insistent hint of dawn
  Fell from the mountain height ;
A wan, uncertain gleam betrayed
  The faltering of the night.

The emphasis of silence made
  The fog above the brook
Intensely pale ; the trees took on
  A haunted, haggard look.

Such quiet came, expectancy
  Filled all the earth and sky :
Time seemed to pause a little space ;
  I heard a dream go by !

SPRING'S TORCH-BEARER.

ORIOLE — athlete of the air —
  Of fire and song a glowing core,
From tropic wildernesses fair,
  Spring's favorite lampadephore,

A hot flambeau on either wing
  Rimples as you pass me by;
'T is seeing flame to hear you sing,
  'T is hearing song to see you fly.

Below the leaves in fragrant gloom,
  Cool currents lead you to your goal,
Where bursting jugs of rich perfume
  Down honeyed slopes of verdure roll.

In eddies, round some hummock cold,
  Where violets weave their azure bredes,
You flash a torch o'er rimy mould
  And rouse the dormant balsam seeds.

Upon the sassafras a flare,
  And through the elm a wavering sheen,
A flicker in the orchard fair,
  A flame across the hedgerow green.

Your voice and light are in my dream
  Of vanished youth, they warm my heart;
With every chirrup, every gleam,
  Sweet currents from old fountains start.

I take me wings and fly with you,
  Once more the boy of long ago.
Oh, days of bloom! Oh, honey-dew!
  Hark! how the flutes of fairy blow!

You whisk wild splendors through the trees,
  And send keen fervors down the wind,
You singe the jackets of the bees,
  And trail an opal mist behind.

When flowery hints foresay the berry,
  On spray of haw and tuft of brier,
Then, wandering incendiary,
  You set the maple swamps afire!

THE ASSAULT.

(*Amazilia cerviniventris.*)

A WINGËD rocket, curving through
  An amethyst trajectory,
Blew up the magazines of dew
  Within the fortress of the bee.

Some say the tulip mortar sent
  The missile forth ; I do not know ;
I scarcely saw which way it went,
  Its whisk of flame surprised me so.

I heard the sudden hum and boom,
  And saw the arc of purple light
Across the garden's rosy gloom ;
  Then something glorious blurred my sight !

The bees forgot to sound alarm,
  And did not pause their gates to lock ;

A topaz terror took by storm
The tower of the hollyhock.

Above the rose a halo hung,
As if a bomb had been a gem,
And round the dahlia's head was swung
A blade that looked a diadem.

What more befell I cannot say;
By ruby glint and emerald gleam
My sense was dazed; the garden lay
Around me like an opal dream!

ODE — SPRING.

PARAPHRASED FROM ANACREON.

When Zephyr on his drooping wings
Soft sighs and spicy fragrance brings,
How sweet to wander on the lawns
Wrapped in the soft green grass of spring
And dewy splendors of the dawns.

How sweet with some dear, blushing maid
To sit in cooling waves of shade
And talk, while o'er her shoulders fair
Falls the full glory of her hair!

LAZING.

Give me a day, let business right itself,
Give me one day to drift in idleness
Along the shores of dreamland. Let me build
My castles in the air and dwell in them
A space, while yet the happy May-winds blow.

The oriole is come, and in the thorn
Among the greening buds the catbird sings;
The fields are sweet, and in the sky is set
A tranquil glory. Let me go and lie
Upon the grass while happy May-winds blow.

I 'd rather rest to-day than be a king,
For what are kings but slaves with golden
chains?
Talk not of work, this is too sweet a day
To bow one's neck and tamely take the yoke,
And I will not, while happy May-winds blow.

This is the month of wooing; let me sit
Close hand in hand with Nature, as a man,
Being deep in love, would sit beside a maid,
And ask for rest as lovers ask for love,
In tender whispers, while the May-winds blow.

And if I fall asleep in Nature's arms,
Like any lover in the arms of love,
Let no one passing by awaken me,
For only once, in all the rolling year,
Comes holiday while happy May-winds blow.

TO A WILD FLOWER.

In the green solitudes
Of the deep, shady woods
Thy lot is kindly cast, and life to thee
Is like a gust of rarest minstrelsy.

The winds of May and June
Hum many a tender tune,
Blowing above thy leafy hiding-place,
Kissing, all thrilled with joy, thy modest face.

About thee float and glow
Rare insects, hovering low,
And round thee glance thin streams of delicate grass,
Plashing their odors on thee as they pass.

The sheen of brilliant wings,
Songs of shy, flitting things,
The low, mysterious melodies that thrill
Through every summer wood, thy sweet life fill.

O bloom ! all joy is thine,
All loves around thee shine ;
The thousand hearts of Nature throb for thee,
Her thousand voices praise thee tenderly.

O bloom of purest glory,
Flower of love's gentlest story,
Forever keep thy petals fresh and fair,
Forever send thy sweetness down the air !

I 'll put thee in my song,
With all thy joys along,
At which some sunny hearts may sunnier grow,
And frozen ones may gently slip their snow.

CERES.

THE wheat was flowing ankle-deep
  Across the field from side to side ;
And, dipping in the emerald waves,
  The swallows flew in circles wide.

The sun, a moment flaring red,
  Shot level rays athwart the world,
Then quenched his fire behind the hills,
  With rosy vapors o'er him curled.

A sweet, insinuating calm, —
  A calm just one remove from sleep,
Such as a tranquil watcher feels,
  Seeing mild stars at midnight sweep

Through splendid purple deeps, and swing
  Their old, ripe clusters down the west
To where, on undiscovered hills,
  The gods have gathered them to rest, —

A calm like that hung over all
  The dusky groves, and, filtered through
The thorny hedges, touched the wheat
  Till every blade was bright with dew.

Was it a dream ? We call things dreams
  When we must needs do so, or own
Belief in old, exploded myths,
  Whose very smoke is long since flown.

Was it a dream ? Mine own eyes saw,
  And Ceres came across the wheat
That, like bright water, dimpled round
  The golden sandals of her feet.

AOEDE.

HER mouth is like a dewy rose
  That blows, but will not open quite;
Like flame turned down, her long hair glows
  In thin, curled currents softly bright;
Her breasts and throat are marble-white.

Her lips will not have any kiss;
  They draw away, they flash a smile, —
Half bashfulness, half scorn it is,
  A silent ripple. . . . All the while
She meditates some charming wile.

Her feet below her drapery shine
  Like roses under clinging sprays,
When, late in summer, lolls the vine; —
  Like flag-leaves in long August days,
To moods perverse her body sways.

Her breath is keen and sweet as nard;
  Her limbs move like a stream flowing

Among smooth stones. A lithe young pard
  Is not more quick than she to spring
To guard or capture anything.

She is a snare, a subtle lure, —
  A lily on a whirlpool's rim.
She is as dangerously pure
  As fire. . . . She revels in a dream
Wherein the daintiest fancies swim.

She feasts upon my pain, and turns
  Her pink ear up to catch my sighs,
And every word I speak. She yearns
  To see me die. . . . Her great gray eyes
Are deep as seas and over-wise.

Ah, over-wise those strange deep eyes!
  They master me, they take my breath;
In them a nameless mystery lies. . . .
  They burn with life that joy bringeth,
They gleam through shining mists of death.

DIANA.

SHE had a bow of yellow horn,
Like the old moon at early morn.

She had three arrows strong and good,
Steel set in feathered cornel wood.

Like purest pearl her left breast shone
Above her kirtle's emerald zone;

Her right was bound in silk well-knit,
Lest her bowstring should sever it.

Ripe lips she had, and clear gray eyes,
And hair pure gold blown hoiden-wise

Across her face, like shining mist
That with dawn's flush is faintly kissed.

Her limbs how matched and round and fine!
How free like song! how strong like wine!

And, timed to music wild and sweet,
How swift her silver-sandaled feet!

Single of heart and strong of hand,
Wind-like she wandered through the land,

No man (or king or lord or churl)
Dared whisper love to that fair girl.

And woe to him who came upon
Her nude, at bath, like Acteon!

So dire his fate that one who heard
The flutter of a bathing bird,

What time he crossed a breezy wood,
Felt sudden quickening of his blood;

Cast one swift look, then ran away
Far through the green, thick groves of May;

Afeard, lest down the wind of spring
He'd hear an arrow whispering!

GARDEN STATUES.

I.

EROS.

O NAKED baby Love among the roses,
Watching with laughing gray-green eyes for me,
Who says that thou art blind? Who hides
from thee?
Who is it in his foolishness supposes
That ever a bandage round thy sweet face
closes
Thicker than gauze? I know that thou canst
see!
Thy glances are more swift and far more sure
To reach their goal than any missile is,
Except that one which never yet did miss,
Whose slightest puncture not even death can
cure,
Whose stroke divides the heart with such a bliss
As even the strongest trembles to endure, —

Thine arrow that makes glad the saddest weather
With the keen rustle of its purple feather!

II.

APHRODITE.

And thou whose tresses like straw-colored gold
Above the scarlet gladiole float and shine, —
Whose comely breasts, whose shoulders fair and fine,
Whose fathomless eyes and limbs of heavenly mould,
Thrill me with pain and pleasures manifold,
Racy of earth, yet full of fire divine, —
Art thou unclean as that old Paphian dream?
I know thou art not; for thou camest to me
Out of the white foam-lilies of the sea,
Out of the salt-clear fountain's clearest stream,
The embodiment of purest purity,
As healthful as the sun's directest beam,
So life-giving that up beneath thy feet,
Wherever thou goest, the grass-flowers bubble sweet!

III.

PSYCHE.

And thou among the violets lying down,
With gracile limbs curled like a sleeping child's,
And dewy lips, and cheeks drawn back with
smiles,
And bright hair wrapped about thee for a gown,
Does some implacable fate with scowl and
frown
Weave for thy feet its dark insidious wiles?
Not so, for I have known thee from thy youth
A singer of sweet tunes and sweeter words,
To merry tinkling of soft cithern chords.
Thine is the way of happiness and truth,
And all thy movements are as swift and smooth
As through the air the strongest flying bird's.
Infinite joy about thy presence clings,
Unspeakable hope falls from thy going wings.

IV.

PERSEPHONE.

And thou that by the poppy bloom dost stand
Robed in the dusky garments of the South,

With slumber in thine eyes and on thy mouth,
Sandaled with silence, having in thy hand
A philter for death and a sleep-bearing wand,
Bringest thou the immitigable fire and drouth?
No; for thy shadowy hair is full of balm,
Thy philter is delight, thy wand gives rest.
See, now I fold my hands upon my breast!
Come, touch me with thy cool and soothing
palm,
Lull me to measureless sleep, ineffable calm,
And bear me to thy garden in the west,
Beyond whose ever-clouded confine lies
A sweet illimitable paradise!

THE TULIP.

(*Caveat regina.*)

Seeing, above dark spikes of green,
  Your great bold flowers of gold and red,
I think of some young heathen queen
  With blazing crown upon her head, —

Some beautiful barbaric thing,
  Clothed in rich garments, emerald zoned,
Whom simple folk, half worshiping
  And half in fear, have crowned and throned.

You will not deign to give the breeze
  The slightest nod as it goes by;
You will not move a leaf to please
  The drowsy gorgeous butterfly.

With measureless nonchalance and pride,
  You take the humming bird's caress;

The brown melodious bee must bide
  Your haughty, arrogant willfulness!

You will not even stoop to hear
  The whisper of the adoring grass;
The violets droop their heads in fear,
  The beetles grumble as they pass.

Beware, O queen, some day ere long
  All these may drop their fealty,
And for redress of causeless wrong
  Uprise in passionate mutiny.

Ah, then what rapturous sound of wings,
  Applauding when your throne goes down!
What cheering when the rude breeze springs,
  And whisks away your withered crown!

WRITTEN ON A FLY-LEAF OF THEOCRITUS.

Those were good times, in olden days,
  Of which the poet has his dreams,
When gods beset the woodland ways,
  And lay in wait by all the streams.

One could be sure of something then
  Severely simple, simply grand,
Or keenly, subtly sweet, as when
  Venus and Love went hand in hand.

Now I would give (such is my need)
  All the world's store of rhythm and rhyme
To see Pan fluting on a reed
  And with his goat-hoof keeping time!

EOS.

SHE stood between two gold pillars ;
  Behind her lay a misty field,
And sunlight smote with great splendor
  Athwart her silver shield.

From her high place she shot an arrow
  That broke the slumber of the sea ;
And one she shot upon a mountain,
  And one flew full at me.

Then the sea began singing, and uplifted
  Its face made glorious for a kiss ;
And the mountain on its green summit
  Built fires of sacrifice.

Then her little feet, gold-sandaled,
  Stepped down the current of a breeze,
And stood upon a river flowing
  Broad like the Euphrates.

And the hills cried, "It is Eos!"
  And the skylark soared away;
And the little fire in the east enkindled,
  Flamed into perfect day!

A BREATH OF MORN.

FLOW in upon my soul, O wind of morn!
Touch me with ancient tenderness and faith,
Thou perfumed waft from fields of blooming corn!
Woo me, lure me from this poisoned shore of Death.

I hear far voices, sweet as flutes, somewhere,
Calling me into the darkness, and I know
Their soft insidious languor on the air
Comes from the land of burial, damp and low.

Blow on me, O thou current of sweet youth!
Come back dear days of boyhood and bright dreams:
Arise again, thou white, clear bloom of truth;
Babble once more, O careless morning streams!

Kiss me, warm lips of purity and love;
Sing to me, lasses from the meadow lands;

Bind me with blossoms from the sacred grove
  Wherein the temple of my childhood stands.

Lo! I am sick to death of Manhood's ways,
  And long to be a fighting man no more;
No more for me the clanging iron days;
  So let me live my happy maytime o'er.

Blow on me, wind, out of the early morn,
  And bear away from me the wear and fret;
Bring me the perfume of the blooming corn,
  And I will sing through many a springtime
      yet!

TWILIGHT.

So short the time, and yet it seems so long,
  Since last I saw thee, O my beautiful!
The very thought is resonant with song,
  And wraps my spirit in a tender lull.

I count the hours till I shall come again:
  Each moment seems a little rose of time;
Each gust of wind thrills gently with a strain
  Of soft, bewildering melody and rhyme.

There comes a perfume from the sunset land,
  And from the sunset vapor comes a voice;
Some one in evening's gateway seems to stand,
  And o'er a flood of glory shout, "Rejoice!"

I seem to look through all the lapsing years,
  And see my path wind through a holy land,
While wondrous as the music of the spheres
  Is the soft murmur of Time's golden sand.

I see my springs go by, a golden train;
 I see my summers with their corn and wines;
I see my autumns come and come again,
 And roar my winters through the windy pines!

SEVEN GOLD REEDS.

SEVEN gold reeds grew tall and slim,
Close by the river's beaded brim.

Syrinx, the naiad, flitted past;
Pan, the goat-hoofed, followed fast.

Oh, such a race was joy to see,
Swift as the flight of bird or bee.

As lightly beat the girl's white feet
They made strange music low and sweet;

So heavily trod the lusty Pan
His hoofs clashed loudly as he ran.

He spread his arms to clasp her there
(Just as she vanished into air),

And to his bosom, warm and rough,
Drew the gold reeds close enough.

Then the wind's low voice began
To hum in the furry ears of Pan.

Out of green bark he made a tether,
And bound seven joints of the reeds together,

And blew a tune so sweet and clear
That all the wild things came to hear.

. . . .

So, to this day, the poet's fire
Springs out of his unslaked desire,

When Love on wingëd feet has fled,
And seven gold reeds are clasped instead!

THE ORPHIC LEGACY.

WHEN steadily blew the wind from shores of Thrace,
And stirred the vines of Lesbos, loaded down
With racy fruit all round Methymna town,
Lo, floating on the water, came a dead man's face.

And from the pallid, parted lips thereof
Issued strange singing of idyllic song,
As it lay tossing white-capped waves among,
Upturned to the sweet sky that smiling bent above.

What wondrous flotsam! And a golden shell
Drifted beside it, stringed with silver chords,
Playing fit accompaniment to the words
That through the sounds of winds and swashing sea did swell.

"Sweetest of all the Ægean Isles," it said,
"Oh, bury me beneath thy fruitful vines,

And pour libations of thy choicest wines;
For, lo, I am the far-famed Thracian singer's
head!

"And I am torn of jealous women's hands,
Because to my dead love I held me true;
Me the Bacchantes, over-drunken, slew;
Now, bodiless, I drift upon thine island sands.

"This my gold shell I bring as gift to thee;
And thou shalt see full soon its precious
use,
When Sappho's voice awakes the lyric
muse,
And with his seven-stringed lute Terpander
charms the sea."

Then through the splendid weather maids
there came,
With loving men, and walked upon the
beach,
Arm twined in arm, and murmuring each to
each,
Slow burning up their hearts in love's sweet,
pitiless flame.

But when the tender gusts of Orphic song
  Smote on their ears with lyre-accompaniment,
  Far down the beach's sandy slope they went,
And found the singing head and tunëd shell among

Sea-drifts that on the foamy surf-line lay.
  What jetsam! but they hailed it with delight;
  They buried the singing head from sight,
And to Methymna took the sweet-stringed shell away.

They hung it in the temple tenderly
  (Where all untouched, its chords kept quivering
  And with rare music never ceased to ring,
That filled the temple as with moanings of the sea).

Thence flaws of song, with charming chords between,
  Swept through the olive groves and dusky vines,

And through the mastic and Aleppo
pines
To the rose-bannered garden walls of Mity-
lene.

PAN IN THE ORCHARD.

He carved a flute of elder green,
  And notched it well and true,
Then pursed his lips and puffed his cheeks
  And merrily he blew.

For it was spring-time holiday,
  A sun-tanned boy was he,
With russet freckles on his face
  And a patch upon his knee.

The apple boughs above him flung
  Their tangled sprays on high,
With one dark, bristly blue-jay nest
  Rough-sketched against the sky.

He knew the secrets of the grass,
  The burden of the hour,
He saw the fierce, bluff bumblebee
  Touse many a clover flower.

Orphaned and poor as poor could be,
  The years before him lay
Dark billows of an unknown sea,
  No light-house on the way.

And yet, and yet his elder flute
  Could bring him comfort true ;
He pursed his lips and puffed his cheeks
  And blew, and blew, and blew !

OUT OF THE SOUTH.

A MIGRANT song-bird I,
Out of the blue, between the sea and the sky,
Landward blown on bright, untiring wings;
Out of the South I fly,
Urged by some vague, strange force of destiny,
To where the young wheat springs,
And the maize begins to grow,
And the clover fields to blow.

I have sought,
In far wild groves below the tropic line,
To lose old memories of this land of mine;
I have fought
This vague, mysterious power that flings me forth
Into the North;
But all in vain. When flutes of April blow
The immemorial longing lures me, and I go.

I go, I go,
The sky above, the sea below,
And I know not by what sense I keep my way,
Slow winnowing the ether night and day;
Yet ever to the same green, fragrant maple grove,
Where I shall swing and sing beside my love,
Some irresistible impulse bears me on,
Through starry dusks and rosy mists of dawn,
And flames of noon and purple films of rain;
And the strain
Of mighty winds hurled roaring back and forth,
Between the caverns of the reeling earth,
Cannot bewilder me.
I know that I shall see,
Just at the appointed time, the dogwood blow,
And hear the willows rustle and the mill-stream flow.

The very bough that best
Shall hold a perfect nest
Now bursts its buds and spills its keen perfume;
And the violets are in bloom,
Beside the boulder, lichen-grown and gray,

Where I shall perch and pipe,
Till the dewberries are ripe,
And our brood has flown away,
And the empty nest swings high
Between the flowing tides of grass and the
dreamy violet sky.

I come, I come!
Bloom, O cherry, peach, and plum!
Bubble brook, and rustle corn and rye!
Falter not, O Nature, nor will I.
Give me thy flower and fruit,
And I 'll blow for thee my flute;
I 'll blow for thee my flute so sweet and clear,
This year,
Next year,
And many and many a blooming coming year,
Till this strange force
No more aloft shall guide me in my course,
High over weltering billows and dark woods,
Over Mississippi's looped and tangled floods,
Over the hills of Tennessee,
And old Kentucky's greenery,
In sun, in night, in clouds, and forth
Out of the South into the North,

To the spot where first the ancestral nest was
swung,
Where first the ancestral song was sung,
Whose shadowy strains still ravish me
With immemorial melody.

A CREOLE SLAVE-SONG.

(*Ah, lo zo-zo chan' dan' branche.*)

What bird is that, with voice so sweet,
  Sings to the sun from yonder tree?
What girl is that so slim and fleet,
Comes through the cane her love to meet?
  Joli zo-zo, sing merrily.
  The pretty girl she comes to me!

What wind is that upon the cane?
  What perfume from a far-off rose
Fills me with dreams? What strange, vague
      pain
Stirs in my heart? What longing vain
  Is this that through my bosom goes?
Oh, south wind, perfume and desire,
You kiss, you soothe, you burn like fire!

Ah, no! Ah, no! It is a cheat.
  There is no bird; my love comes not;

The wind chills me from head to feet,
And oh, it brings no perfume sweet.
  My slender girl the white man bought,
And took her far across the bay —
I cannot cut the cane to-day !

I cannot cut the cane to-day —
  O zo-zo, moqueur, come and sing !
O warm wind, through the cane-field stray,
Wave the long moss so soft and gray !
  I have no heart for anything ;
But life was Heaven and work was play
When my love loved me every day !

White man, how I worked for you,
  When I was young and blithe and strong !
The earth was green, the sky was blue,
My love's eyes were as bright as dew ;
  And life was like the *zo-zo's* song !
But you — you sold my love away —
I cannot cut the cane to-day !

I did not dream a slave could be
  A man, and right a grievous wrong.

I writhed and bore your cruelty;
I felt the soul go out of me;
  And yet, I was so lion-strong
I could have torn your heart away —
I cannot cut the cane to-day!

Freedom! I feel it when too late,
  Like Spring wind on a blasted tree,
A waft of mockery and hate!
Bring back my chains, O cruel Fate!
  Bring youth and slavery back to me;
Bring back the lash, the hound, the pain,
So that my own love come again!

But hark! A gentle voice afar
  Calls me to go, I know not where —
Yes, past the sun and past the star,
Into God's land. A golden car
  And milk-white horses — *she* is there!
So sweet — I dream — I float away —
I cannot cut the cane to-day!

A MORNING PRAYER.

O breeze!
Thou dewy, cool, sweet current of delight,
Appease
This longing for the ripe fruit of the right;
Winnow my soul
And flood my heart's cold caves with charity,
And roll
This burden of the love of sin from me!

O sky!
Pour thy vast cup of purity on me,
That I
May sound the flawless note of liberty,
As I stand
Waiting to see the flower of sunrise blow,
Waiting to feel the fresher currents flow
Into this morning land.

O sea!
Thou weltering giant, lend thy stormy voice
To me,

That I this day may make the earth rejoice
With a sky-filling, world-o'erwhelming song,
The tempest song of Freedom blowing down
the walls of Wrong!

Lord God!
Thou master of the winds, the skies, the seas,
Who trod
The valley of man's lowest miseries,
Lend me thy love, that I may love all men,
That I may show all men the way of love,
From palace high to deepest prison-den;
That I may prove
How Brotherhood is Freedom's other name,
How Freedom's other name is but the Word,
And that Word is the Lord
Come down again.
Amen.

FULL-FLEDGED.

(*Une barbe de jeune dieu.*)

Is all discovery made?
Is the hand of Conquest stayed?
Are all the heroes dead, all epics told?
Is Fame's grand tower no more
On any height or shore?
Is the bard's Excalibur worn thin and dull and
old?

O for a sweet, strange waft —
A thrilling, hopeful draught
From a land where no man's feet were ever
set;
Where nameless wild birds sing,
And the woods and everything
With fragrant, honey-flavored dews are wet!

We build our ships in vain,
If no new shores we gain.
Though back and forth we track that Genoese

Who found fresh, wholesome room
For Freedom's root and bloom,
Yet shall we long to sail the unknown seas!

Where shall I lay my head?
What grass shall be my bed?
What holy, unsullied grove shall shadow me?
Somewhere, somewhere I know,
Untasted fountains flow
And winds blow off an undiscovered sea!

The clarion is whist;
No knight rides down the list;
High courage is but dust on rusted shields;
Where grandest deeds were done,
Most glorious battles won,
Dull peasants plow in poor and arid fields.

Old Homer and old wine,
And Shakespeare the divine,
And women for whose sake the world was changed, —
All these are of the past;
Romance has breathed her last;
Genius, with lamp and lyre, through every grove has ranged.

The jaded worshipers,
The priests and followers
Of the high God, no fresh gift-offerings bring
From full-fed flocks and herds,
But, mumbling unmeaning words,
Burn fleshless bones and impotent censers swing.

Love walks not anywhere ;
Venus, no longer fair,
Into some lonely place has crept away ;
The dryad and the fawn
And the river-gods are gone,
And in the woods no more the lusty satyrs stray.

But my young limbs are strong,
My throat thirsts for a song !
The meanings and the potencies of youth
Are gathering in my reins
And throbbing in my veins ;
I pant and pine for deep clean springs of Truth !

I will not have the lute,
Nor that old, worm-bitten flute
Bequeathed by gods to the dull line of bards.

Charmed reeds of song there are
By happy streams afar,
And I shall cut mine own, despite what demon
guards !

Ready, clear-eyed, alert,
Mine own I shall assert,
Repeating no man's manner, no man's note ;
But gathering from primal sources
The pure and subtle forces
That shall with rarest resonance flood my throat.

I cannot stand and wait
I have no faith in Fate.
The sinews of my body, lithe and clean,
Promise a better turn
Than all the stars that burn,
As o'er Morn's outmost rosy rim I lean.

I will not look behind ;
But down some brisk, sharp wind,
Exulting, into the future I shall spring,
Brown-limbed, anointed, free,
To breast swift floods and see
What wider view Time's highest tide shall bring !

I shall not tire or fail ;
Strange essence shall exhale
(Suggesting life immortal) from my song,
And all the world shall smile,
Half-owning for a while
The influence of the healthful and the strong !

I shall break every chain,
To farthest heights attain,
And drink from wells no face has bent above.
Oh ! from what heavenly place
Shall leap to my embrace
The warm embodiment of innocent love ?

THE FINAL THOUGHT.

WHAT is the grandest thought
Toward which the soul has wrought?
Has it the epic form,
And the power of a storm?
Comes it of prophecy
(That borrows light of uncreated fires),
Or of transmitted strains of memory
Sent down through countless sires?

I tiptoe on the verge
Of the Future, and I urge
Into vast space the cry of my despair
(Which, like a sea-gull lost in upper air,
Glides weakly on and on);
But whither is it gone,
This straying cry with human anguish fraught?
What is the final thought?

Which way are my feet set?
Through infinite changes yet

Shall I go on,
Nearer and nearer drawn
To Thee,
God of eternity?
How shall the human grow,
By changes fine and slow,
To Thy perfection from the life-dawn sought?
What is the highest thought?

Ah, these dim memories
Of when Thy voice spake lovingly to me,
Under the Eden trees,
Saying: "Lord of all creation thou shalt be,"
How they haunt me and elude —
How they hover, how they brood,
On the horizon, fading yet dying not!
What is the final thought?

What if I once did dwell
In the lowest dust germ-cell,
A faint fore-hint of life called forth of God,
Waxing and struggling on,
Through the long, flickering dawn,
The awful while His feet earth's bosom trod?

What if He shaped me so,
And caused my life to blow
Into the full soul-flower in Eden-air?
Lo! now I am not good,
And I stand in solitude,
Calling to Him (and yet He answers not):
What is the final thought?

What myriads of years up from the germ!
What countless ages back from man to worm!
And yet from man to God, oh help me now!
A cold despair is beading on my brow!
I may see Him, and seeing know Him not!
What is the highest thought?

Oh, higher than the skies
My ecstatic prayers arise!
The stars hear them go by
Into the regions of Eternity—
The angels meet them wandering after Him,
Begging for just one ray
Of perfect light across the spaces dim
To guide me on my long and lonely way.

Oh, lead me, I am blind!
Back, back, until I find
The rapture-haunted spot,
Where still the all-creative Essence fills
Forms (out of dead clay wrought)
With godlike souls and heaven-aspiring wills —
Back to the highest thought!

A fragrant breath goes by;
A subtile waft, from some far paradise,
Blows on me fitfully,
And colors, half unseen, allure my eyes,
All sightless though they be;
And so my heart is filled with wild desire,
And all my soul is like a flaring fire!
What is this flame in which my life is caught?
Is it the highest thought?

"Blasphemer, hush!
The universe would rush
To be a part of thee, if thou couldst know
The garden where God's flowers of wisdom blow!
Cry not to Him
Across the spaces dim;

Dare not to touch His ether with thy breath,
Thou bearer of the ancient curse of death !
Prayer shall avail thee not :
Shrink from the final thought ! "

So comes, at last,
The answer from the Vast. . . .
Not so, there is a rush of wings —
Earth feels the presence of invisible things,
Closer and closer drawn
In fragrant mists of dawn !
One dies to conquer Death
And to burst the awful tomb, —
Lo, with His dying breath
He blows love into bloom !
Love ! faith is born of it !
Death is the scorn of it !
It fills the earth and thrills the heaven above,
And God is love,
And life is love, and, though we heed it not,
Love is the final thought.

NECTAR AND AMBROSIA.

If I were a poet, my sweetest song
Should have the bouquet of scuppernong,
With a racy smack in every line
From the savage juice of the muscadine.

The russet persimmon, the brown papaw,
The red wild plum and the summer haw,
Serviceberries and mandrake fruit,
Sassafras bark and ginseng root,
Should make my verse pungent and sweet by turns;
And the odor of grass and the freshness of ferns,
The kernels of nuts and the resins of trees,
The nectar distilled by the wild honey-bees,
Should be thrown in together, to flavor my words
With the zest of the woods and the joy of the birds!

Who sings by note, from the page of a book,
So sweet a tune as the brawl of a brook?
Shall Homer, or shall Anacreon
Suggest as much as the wind or the sun?

Give me a shell from the sea so green,
Cut me a flute from the Aulocrene,
Give me Nature's sweets and sours,
Her barks and nuts, her fruits and flowers;
And all the music I make shall be
Good as the sap of the maple-tree,
Whilst a rare bouquet shall fill my song
From the muscadine and the scuppernong.

A DREAM OF ROMANCE.

THE day is but a breezy dream,
  The sky is like a bloom ;
Life flows, a fragrant, bubbling stream,
  Along a lilied flume.

The wandering butterfly is lost
  In films of mystery,
From supple flower to flower is tossed
  The worried bumblebee.

On high some idle spirit sings,
  Half sleeping, as it flies,
Dropping from its charmëd wings
  The dews of Paradise.

The pines are dozing, and the sea
  Is murmuring in its sleep ;
All round the sky rim drowsily
  Some shadowy wonders creep.

The mosses drop their curtains low,
  The far ships settle down,
And tenderly the Gulf winds blow,
  O'er Bay Saint Louis town.

And lo! am I a mote to dance
  And shimmer here and there,
Where faded beams of old romance
  Strike slantwise through the air.

A weltering sound, remote and vast,
  Comes to my drowsy ear;
The Gulf waves rolling from the past
  Suggest the buccaneer.

A corsair sloop, hull down, retires
  With mysteries in her hold;
Her sails, against the wizard fires
  Of morn, are torn and old.

The buccaneer! The buccaneer!
  My boyhood dreams come true;
What wild uproar is this I hear
  Across the waters blue?

"Welcome! my brawny, bearded one,
  Salute!" the caverns boom,
And the merchantmen, far scattered, run
  To give his ship sea room.

He answers with a growling throat;
  Out leaps his rusty blade,
And one dull, echoing thunder-note
  Bounds from the carronade.

Lo! all the world stands by to gaze
  And lean and look askance,
What time the sturdy tars upraise
  The banner of romance.

Merrily, merrily, sing the crew;
  Dusky and grim are they,
Against the islands soft and blue
  And the grizzly ocean spray.

What is her name? What is her name?
  This ship so dark and strong.
Oh, she was christened Lady Fame,
  And built by King o' Song.

And she was manned by frowzy men,
  Bohemians eke, who love
To fight at odds, like one to ten,
  And reck not where they rove.

And who is captain, tell us true,
  Of this good Lady Fame?
Shouts every tar of all the crew:
  "WILL SHAKESPEARE is his name!"

Oh, welcome, goodly ship, in haste
  To bring us prize and cheer
From all the hoards that tempt the taste
  Of lawless buccaneer!

Ay, we will build us crafts galore,
  Like Shakespeare's they shall be,
And we will plunder every shore
  And every ship at sea.

All round the deep, wave-tossed and blown,
  Led by the Lady Fame,
Our fleet shall make the world its own,
  Reckless of shame or blame.

The South, the North, the East, the West,
  Our shout and rout shall hear;
Oh, who shall foil, or who arrest
  The ruthless buccaneer?

'T was thus I dreamed, one balmy day,
  When dim ships went, hull down,
Against the sky line far away,
  Off Bay Saint Louis town.

There sapphire islands, held aloof
  In films of dream and chance,
Between sea floor and blue sky roof,
  Are steeped in wild romance.

So in this town I linger long,
  And watch and wait — alack!
Never a breath of golden song
  Can blow the old time back!

Oh, leave me thus, a mote to dance
  And shimmer here and there,
Where faded beams of old romance
  Strike slantwise through the air!

IN THE HAUNTS OF BASS AND BREAM.

I.

DREAMS come true, and everything
Is fresh and lusty in the spring.

In groves that smell like ambergris,
Wind-songs, bird-songs, never cease.

Go with me down by the stream,
Haunt of bass and purple bream;

Feel the pleasure, keen and sweet,
When the cool waves lap your feet;

Catch the breath of moss and mould,
Hear the grosbeak's whistle bold;

See the heron all alone
Midstream on a slippery stone,

Or, on some decaying log,
Spearing snail or water-frog.

See the shoals of sun-perch shine
Among the pebbles smooth and fine,

Whilst the sprawling turtles swim
In the eddies cool and dim!

II.

The busy nuthatch climbs his tree,
Around the great bole spirally,

Peeping into wrinkles gray,
Under ruffled lichens gay,

Lazily piping one sharp note
From his silver mailëd throat;

And down the wind the catbird's song
A slender medley trails along.

Here a grackle chirping low,
There a crested vireo;

Deep in tangled underbrush
Flits the shadowy hermit-thrush ;

Coos the dove, the robin trills,
The crows caw from the airy hills ;

Purple finch and pewee gray,
Bluebird, swallow, oriole gay, —

Every tongue of Nature sings ;
The air is palpitant with wings.

Halcyon prophecies come to pass
In the haunts of bream and bass.

III.

Bubble, bubble, flows the stream,
Like an old tune through a dream.

Now I cast my silken line ;
See the gay lure spin and shine,

While with delicate touch I feel
The gentle pulses of the reel.

Halcyon laughs and cuckoo cries;
Through its leaves the plane-tree sighs.

Bubble, bubble, flows the stream,
Here a glow and there a gleam;

Coolness all about me creeping,
Fragrance all my senses steeping, —

Spicewood, sweet-gum, sassafras,
Calamus and water-grass,

Giving up their pungent smells,
Drawn from Nature's secret wells;

On the cool breath of the morn,
Perfume of the cock-spur thorn,

Green spathes of the dragon-root,
Indian turnip's tender shoot,

Dogwood, red-bud, elder, ash,
Snowy gleam and purple flash,

Hillside thickets, densely green,
That the partridge revels in!

IV.

I see the morning-glory's curl,
The curious star-flower's pointed whorl ;

Hear the woodpecker, rap-a-tap !
See him with his cardinal's cap !

And the querulous, leering jay,
How he clamors for a fray !

Patiently I draw and cast,
Keenly expectant till, at last,

Comes a flash, down in the stream,
Never made by perch or bream ;

Then a mighty weight I feel, —
Sings the line and whirs the reel !

V.

Out of a giant tulip-tree
A great gay blossom falls on me ;

Old gold and fire its petals are,
It flashes like a falling star.

A big blue heron flying by
Looks at me with a greedy eye.

I see a striped squirrel shoot
Into a hollow maple root;

A bumblebee with mail all rust,
And thighs puffed out with anther-dust,

Clasps a shrinking bloom about,
And draws her amber sweetness out.

VI.

Bubble, bubble, flows the stream,
Like a song heard in a dream.

A white-faced hornet hurtles by,
Lags a turquoise butterfly, —

One intent on prey and treasure,
One afloat on tides of pleasure!

Sunshine arrows, swift and keen,
Pierce the burr-oak's helmet green.

VII.

I follow where my victim leads
Through tangles of rank water-weeds,

O'er stone and root and knotty log,
O'er faithless bits of reedy bog.

I wonder, will he ever stop?
The reel hums like a humming top!

Through graceful curves he sweeps the line,
He sulks, he starts, his colors shine,

Whilst I, all flushed and breathless, tear
Through lady-fern and maidenhair,

And in my straining fingers feel
The throbbing of the rod and reel!

A thin sandpiper, wild with fright,
Goes into ecstasies of flight;

A gaunt green bittern quits the rushes,
The yellow-throat its warbling hushes;

Bubble, bubble, flows the stream,
Like an old tune through a dream!

VIII.

At last he tires, I reel him in;
I see the glint of scale and fin.

The crinkled halos round him break,
He leaves gay bubbles in his wake.

I raise the rod, I shorten line,
And safely land him, — he is mine!

IX.

The belted halcyon laughs, the wren
Comes twittering from his bushy den;

The turtle sprawls upon its log,
I hear the booming of a frog.

Liquidambar's keen perfume,
Sweet-punk, calamus, tulip-bloom;

Dancing wasp and dragon-fly,
Wood-thrush whistling tenderly;

Damp cool breath of moss and mould,
Noontide's influence manifold;

Glimpses of a cloudless sky, —
Soothe me as I resting lie.

Bubble, bubble, flows the stream,
Like low music through a dream.

TO A REALIST.

A crossbow old, with lathe and gaffle grim,
And carven stock, hung in a castle hall —
Mere bricabrac, but on the distance dim
It sketched De Jourdan's quarrel, Richard's fall.

A curious ballad written by Villon
(The sweet old thief) — the page was wan and sere;
But genius had set a glow thereon
Like memory's flush on snows that fell last year.

A broken plow beside a hedgerow flung
Amid the flowering weeds of early June,
Told of poor Burns, who from the furrow sung
The "Banks of Ayr" and "Braes o' Bonnie Doon."

A fossil skeleton, delicate and rare,
  A bird (held fast in rock for ages long)
Freed by the quarrymen. I heard the air
  Eons ago thrill to its morning song!

A southern zittern found at Avignon;
  Broken its keys with pearls and opals set;
Its strings were rust, its wreathëd sound-board gone,
  But chords of passion wrung it fret by fret.

A leathern bottle, wrinkled, black and old,
  And dry as dust of Eden's apple bloom —
Ah, but the philter that it used to hold
  Haunted it with the ghost of strange perfume.

A phrase by Sappho, or a violin
  Made at Cremona — all the bits of clay
That Palissy burned deathless color in —
  The crudest charcoal sketches of Millet, —

How rich in charm, how redolent and ripe
  And fertile is the purple mood they bring!

The heroes fight again, Pan blows his pipe,
  And from the sacred groves the Muses sing.

Time spares the germs that subtle genius needs ;
  Forth from the blue of distance they are sent ;
And poor indeed is he who never heeds
  What precious hints fall from the firmament.

Aloft, arear, in caverns dark, profound,
  Where no dull commonplace has ever been,
The golden web of genius is wound,
  Which all the thronging world is tangled in.

Genius, that wind-worn reed, unsightly, rude,
  Notched by some strong, untutored artisan ;
That golden lyre, that lute of jeweled wood,
  That syrinx blown by furry lips of Pan !

Ah, friend, as you read Keats one starry night,
  While on the world lay dreams and mystery,
You felt a thrill, trembled, and cried outright :
  " Young god ! Strange boy ! Let go the
      heart of me ! "

AMERICA.

Low-hung in darkness, steeped in tyranny,
  The earth was but a prison-pen for man,
When a swift impulse leaped from sea to sea,
  And round the sodden zones a flash of fervor
    ran.

A throb of God's great heart with sympathy
  Shook all the world. The torn sky and the
    stars
Draped the majestic form of Liberty,
  The while around the West she built her
    golden bars.

There was a sound of thunder rolling far,
  When Freedom's forest-altar was begun,
A song of star that answered unto star,
  When Freedom's heaven-high temple in the
    West was done!

Done? Oh, never done! the builder buildeth fair,
Stone upon stone, that all the world may know;
Higher and higher, in purer veins of air,
The parapets of love, the towers of beauty grow.

The slave whose ear feels yet the post and nail,
The serf in some Siberian hell, the oppressed
Of rack-rent, and the debtor in the jail,
All pray with hopeful faces yearning to the West.

Reality of life's divine romance
Befalls what time the broken chains crash down;
And lo! full manhood, leaping from a trance
Shakes off the chrysalis shell of trodden clod and clown.

Oh, brothers, come! The breath of heaven is here!
One draught can make the slave and master one!

The grace of liberty softens year by year,
  And in a richer flood the stream of life flows
    on.

But come not here to batter and debase,
  Nor hoping to reach license unconfined;
No alien hand our inscriptions may efface,
  Justice may be, but vigilant Freedom is not,
    blind!

Come rather as the bridegroom to the bride,
  Or as a man made free to freeborn man,
Love-blown across the ocean wild and wide,
  Upon our shores, to be a true American!

And join our song, oh, every alien tongue,
  Make thunder-music on our highest wall,
While hearts of kings are faint and terror-wrung,
  And all the olden thrones are toppling to
    their fall!

America, new gospel bearer, hail!
  Thou second coming of the loving Lord!
Thy thousand years of glory cannot fail,
  Thou dewy, bloom-sweet resurrection of
    God's word!

Thy destiny the Father's fingers wove,
The spell of power is on thee. Sweet and strong
Flames in thine eyes the fire of heavenly love,
And from thy brimming heart leaps love's immortal song!

AN ADDRESS

BY AN EX-CONFEDERATE SOLDIER, TO THE GRAND ARMY OF THE REPUBLIC.

I.

I WAS a rebel, if you please,
  A reckless fighter to the last,
Nor do I fall upon my knees
  And ask forgiveness for the past.

A traitor? *I* a traitor? No!
  I was a patriot to the core;
The South was mine, I loved her so,
  I gave her all, — I could no more.

You scowl at me. And was it wrong
  To wear the gray my father wore?
Could I slink back, though young and strong,
  From foes before my mother's door?

My mother's kiss was hot with fight,
  My father's frenzy filled his son,

Through reeking day and sodden night
  My sister's courage urged me on.

And I, a missile steeped in hate,
  Hurled forward like a cannon-ball
By the resistless hand of fate,
  Rushed wildly, madly through it all.

I stemmed the level flames of hell,
  O'er bayonet bars of death I broke,
I was so near when Cleburne fell,
  I heard the muffled bullet stroke!

But all in vain. In dull despair
  I saw the storm of conflict die;
Low lay the Southern banner fair,
  And yonder flag was waving high.

God, what a triumph had the foe!
  Laurels, arches, trumpet-blare;
All around the earth their songs did go,
  Thundering through heaven their shouts did
    tear.

My mother, gray and bent with years,
  Hoarding love's withered aftermath,

Her sweet eyes burnt too dry for tears,
  Sat in the dust of Sherman's path.

My father, broken, helpless, poor,
  A gloomy, nerveless giant stood,
Too strong to cower and endure,
  Too weak to fight for masterhood.

My boyhood's home, a blackened heap
  Where lizards crawled and briers grew,
Had felt the fire of vengeance creep,
  The crashing round-shot hurtle through.

I had no country, all was lost,
  I closed my eyes and longed to die,
While past me stalked the awful ghost
  Of mangled, murdered Liberty.

The scars upon my body burned,
  I felt a heel upon my throat,
A heel that ground and grinding turned
  With each triumphal trumpet note.

"Grind on!" I cried, "nor doubt that I,
  (If all your necks were one and low

As mine is now) delightedly
  Would cut it by a single blow!"

II.

That was dark night; but day is here,
  The crowning victory is won;
Hark, how the sixty millions cheer,
  With Freedom's flag across the sun!

I a traitor! Who are *you*
  That dare to breathe that word to me?
You never wore the Union blue,
  No wounds attest *your* loyalty!

I do detest the sutler's clerk,
  Who skulked and dodged till peace had come,
Then found it most congenial work
  To beat the politician's drum.

I clasp the hand that made my scars,
  I cheer the flag my foemen bore,
I shout for joy to see the stars
  All on our common shield once more.

I do not cringe before you now,
  Or lay my face upon the ground ;
I am a man, of men a peer,
  And not a cowering, cudgeled hound !

I stand and say that you were right,
  I greet you with uncovered head,
Remembering many a thundering fight,
  Where whistling death between us sped.

Remembering the boys in gray,
  With thoughts too deep and fine for words,
I lift this cup of love to-day
  To drink what only love affords.

Soldiers in blue, a health to you !
  Long life and vigor oft renewed,
While on your hearts, like honey-dew,
  Falls our great country's gratitude.

AN INCIDENT OF WAR.

OUR new flagbearer, pale and slim,
  A beardless youth of quiet mien,
Much chaffed at by old soldiers grim
  (Before in battle he had been),
Hid the heroic fire in him.

He sang old hymns and prayed at night;
  "A bad sign," quoth the sergeant bold,
"Camp-meeting tunes before a fight
  Loosen a soldier's moral hold,
And pluck beats prayer a mighty sight."

The boy blushed red, but tenderly
  He to the sergeant turned and said:
"That God should mind me what am I?
  And yet by Him my soul is fed —
Send this to mother if I die."

The sergeant, with a knowing look,
  And winking at the rest, replied:

"Yes, son, I 'll give your ma the book" —
  Just then a volley rattled wide
And one great gun the valley shook.

The pale flagbearer disappeared.
  "Gone to the rear," the sergeant said;
"Praying would make a Turk afeared;
  Those lonesome tunes have turned his
      head" —
And then the tide of battle neared.

We formed in haste and dashed away,
  Across the field, our place to fill;
At first a skirmish, then a spray
  Of cannon smoke upon a hill
Flanked by long lines in close array.

Down charged the foe; we rushed to meet,
  We filled the valley like a sea,
The cannons flashed a level sheet
  Of blinding flame, the musketry
Cut men as sickles cut the wheat!

Oh, then we shouted! More and more
  The fervor of our courage rose,

As through our solid columns tore
  The death hail's crashing, gusty blows,
And louder leaped the cannon roar!

But how could human courage meet
  That icy flood? All, all in vain
Our counter charge; in slow retreat
  We crossed the tumbled heaps of slain,
With grave-pits yawning at our feet!

"Rally! For shame!" rang out a cry
  Forth from the thundering vortex cast;
A voice so steady, clear, and high,
  It sounded like a bugle-blast
Blown from the lips of victory.

We paused, took hope, yelled loud, and so
  Renewed the charge, all as one man,
Leaped where Death's waves had thickest flow,
  And felt the breath of horror fan
Our naked souls as cold as snow!

The volleys quickened, coalesced,
  Rolled deep, rocked earth and jarred the sky,

When lo! our banner bearer pressed
  His standard forward, held it high
And rode upon the battle's crest.

We saw him wave it over all;
  Caught in the battle trough and dashed
From side to side, it would not fall;
  But like a meteor danced and flashed
And reveled in the sulphurous pall!

We swept the field and won the hill;
  Our flag flared out upon the crest,
Where wavering, gasping, pale and chill,
  A dozen bullets through his breast,
The slender hero held it still!

We leaped to lift his drooping head,
  The sergeant clasped him to his breast;
"I bore the flag," the low voice said,
  "And God bore me, now let me rest,"
And so we laid him with the dead.

TO THE SOUTH.

O SUBTLE, musky, slumbrous clime!
  O swart, hot land of pine and palm,
Of fig, peach, guava, orange, lime,
  And terebinth and tropic balm!
Land where our Washington was born,
When truth in hearts of gold was worn;
Mother of Marion, Moultrie, Lee,
Widow of fallen chivalry!
No longer sadly look behind,
But turn and face the morning wind,
And feel sweet comfort in the thought:
  "*With each fierce battle's sacrifice*
  I sold the wrong at awful price,
And bought the good; but knew it not."

Cheer up! Reach out! Breathe in new life!
Brood not on unsuccessful strife
Against the current of the age;
The Highest is thy heritage!

Leave off this death's-head scowl at Fate,
And into thy true heart sink this :
" *God loves to walk where Freedom is !*"

There is no sweet in dregs and lees ;
There is no fruit on girdled trees.
Plant new vineyards, sow new fields,
For bread and wine the Future yields ;
Out of free soil fresh spathes shall start ;
Now is the budding-time of Art !

But hark ! O hear ! My senses reel !
Some grand presentiment I feel !
A voice of love, bouquet of truth,
The quick sound of the feet of youth !

Lo ! from the war-cloud, dull and dense,
  Loyal and chaste and brave and strong,
Comes forth the South with frankincense,
  And vital freshness in her song.
The weight is fallen from her wings ;
To find a purer air she springs
Out of the Night into the Morn,
Fair as cotton, sound as corn.

Hold! Shall a Northman, fierce and grim,
With hoary beard and boreal vim,
Thus fling, from some bleak waste of ice,
Frost-crystals of unsought advice
  To those who dwell by Coosa's stream,
Or on dark hummocks plant the cane
Beside the lovely Pontchartrain,
  Or in gay sail-boats drift and dream
Where Caribbean breezes stray
On Pensacola's drowsy bay?

Not so! I am a Southerner;
I love the South; I dared for her
To fight from Lookout to the sea,
With her proud banner over me:
But from my lips thanksgiving broke,
As God in battle thunder spoke,
And that Black Idol, breeding drouth
And dearth of human sympathy
Throughout the sweet and sensuous South,
  Was, with its chains and human yoke,
Blown hellward from the cannon's mouth,
  While Freedom cheered behind the smoke!

OUR LEGEND.

THE legend set upon our shield
  Brims with grand meaning: All in one,
  Hearts welded, souls together run
At white heat on the battlefield!

One shining way for all to take,
  One oath, one hope, one purpose grand,
  One flag for all in all the land,
Upheld by all for Freedom's sake.

One sign set in the central sky,
  Read of all men alike, a name
  Written in empyrean flame
By the bold hand of Destiny!

That legend naught could dim or mar;
  Though bathed in tears and hid in smoke,
  Forth from the focal storm it broke,
A bow above the cloud of war.

We read it pensively and knew
  Some element of precious gain
  Had come to it from wounds and pain,
And mightily its meaning grew.

And so we keep upon our shield
  The deathless legend: All in one,
  Hearts welded, souls together run
At white heat on the battlefield.

A myriad songs, together thrown
  Across old gulfs of hate, are blent
  Like starlight in the firmament,
And round the world in triumph blown.

Our starry unity of stars
  Gives man a manly masterhood,
  Our law of love engrossed in blood
Is sealed with burning bullet scars!

A TAUNT.

In the oldest wood I know a brooklet,
  That bubbles over stones and roots,
And ripples out of hollow places,
  Like music out of flutes.

There creeps the pungent breath of cedars,
  Rich coolness wraps the air about,
Whilst through clear pools electric flashes
  Betray the watchful trout.

I know where wild things lurk and linger,
  In groves as gray and grand as Time;
I know where God has written poems
  Too strong for words or rhyme.

Come, let us go, each pulse is precious,
  Come, ere the day has lost its dawn;
And you shall quaff life's finest essence
  From primal flagons drawn!

Just for a day slip off the tether
  Of hothouse wants, and dare to be
A child of Nature, strong and simple,
  Out in the woods with me.

Out in the woods, on freedom's bosom,
  We shall be worthy sons of men,
Bred of remotest sires who bearded
  The satyr in his den.

Come, just a sip of the wild man's nectar
  Shall show you life from a point of view
As old as the oldest stones of the mountains,
  And yet as fresh as dew!

Supple joints and bulging muscles,
  Sinews taut as the chords of a harp,
Veins full-flushed, eyes clear as water,
  And all the senses sharp.

Who was Shakespeare? Where is Homer?
  Can Milton leap, or dance, or run?
Should you care to cast a fly with Walton?
  Do you envy Napoleon?

What of this lore of buried thinkers?
  What of these classic depths and heights?
Better one strong, bright, living creature
  Than a myriad trilobites!

Ah, I see you scoff at my meaning,
  You flaccid, indolent bookworm, you!
What would you give for my good digestion
  And my nerve-cords sound and true?

MORNING DEW.

WHEN germs were quickening in the mould,
  And sap was rich and leaves were young,
Deep in the fragrant wood a lute,
  As old as Time, was newly strung.

Some swift, divine, invisible hand,
  From fret to fret, tried all the chords,
Until a tune, supremely sweet,
  Was set to immemorial words.

And then the wild bird sought its mate;
  The lusty bee a-booming came;
The maples, filled with racy pangs,
  Let go their buds' imprisoned flame;

A dreamy mystery veiled the sun;
  Keen perfumes stole through glade and
      grove,
And all the founts of Nature burst
  With sudden bubbling streams of love!

Ah! passion, pure as morning dew,
  And fresh as breath of mint and thyme!
Impulse of Spring, so new and true!
  Essence of innocence and prime!

I bowed my head and stilled my breath
  (For it was May and I was young),
While to a tune supremely sweet
  Those immemorial words were sung.

OLD ROCHON.

I.

It was off the coast of the Terre aux Bœufs
(And the breeze was brisk and the sea was
rough)
That Gaspard Rochon, the buccaneer,
Sailed his schooner, and right good cheer
Had he on his table, with pipes and wine,
As he feasted the mate of the Caroline.

II.

The Caroline was a cruiser craft ;
Rochon had raked her fore and aft,
With cannon and with carronade,
And had boarded her with pike and blade,
Had pillaged and sunk her ; only the mate
Was left to tell of his vessel's fate.

III.

" You fought like a tiger," said old Rochon,
" And I 'll bet my schooner, the Gonfalon,

That you have heard the broadsides roar
And the cutlasses clang ofttimes before."
"Yes," growled the mate, "for many a year
I 've battled with pirate and buccaneer."

IV.

"Drink and be merry," the outlaw said;
Drink to the living and drink to the dead.
Drink pale sherry and drink old port!
Eat and be merry, for life is short!
Ay, drink like a fish and eat like a swine,
For death may follow when pirates dine!"

V.

"By the way," said the mate, "did you ever
hear
Of old Rochon, the buccaneer,
Who used to sail the southern seas,
With his rendezvous in the Florida keys?"
"Perchance I have," was the curt reply,
With a savage gleam from the old man's eye.

VI.

"He was a terror," the mate went on,
(All unaware that he faced Rochon)

"A cut-throat villain, a coward, too,
With a stolen ship and a dastard crew; —
But his race is ended, he 's feared no more
By women and children on sea or shore."

VII.

Over the mate, from head to heel,
The pirate outflung a glance of steel.
"Gaspard Rochon was a buccaneer
Who never felt a touch of fear,"
He said, "and I 'd like to drink a cup
With the tar who broke his cruising up!"

VIII.

"Well," said the mate, "I ran him down,
Burnt his vessels and razed his town;
Women and men, every devil's one,
I killed of the gang, save old Rochon,
Who made escape with loss of an ear."
"And who cut that?" roared the buccaneer.

IX.

"Who but I?" sang out the mate.
"My cutlass glanced from his flinty pate
And shaved his ear off, close and clean,

Which I have in my pouch as dry as a bean."
"Show me," the old man stormed, "that ear
Of old Rochon the buccaneer!"

X.

"Here it is," said the mate with pride,
As out of the pouch that hung by his side
He drew the relic and held it high,
Like a bit of parchment brown and dry.
"Ha! ha! ha!" laughed the buccaneer,
"Eat and drink and have good cheer!

XI.

"Drink pale sherry and drink red port!
Eat and be merry, for life is short!"
And then he hurried the mate on deck
And tied a halliard around his neck,
While the crew stood by to haul away,
And a hunchback fifer began to play.

XII.

For years the schooner Gonfalon
Was sailed by the savage old Rochon,
And wherever she went, at her topmast high
Dangled a corpse against the sky—

A corpse that like a mummy grew
And lightly about in the breezes blew!

XIII.

Oh, red were the deeds of old Rochon
And wild were the crew of the Gonfalon!
In every nook of the Spanish main
The cruisers cruised for them in vain,
While they robbed and feasted and drank good
wine
To the health of the mate of the Caroline!

A STUDY FOR THE CRITICS.

A GREAT king once, so I have heard,
Went out to hunt a singing-bird
Whose voice should be so sweet and strong,
So fraught with all the tricks of song,
That they who heard it would confess
The king's fine taste and perfectness
Of judgment. And it came to pass
That where the wind poured through the grass,
Fringing a brooklet's sinuous way,
He saw a bird demure and gray,
Of awkward mien and sleepy eyed,
Bathing in the crystal tide.

"O bird!" the king said, looking down,
"A monarch I of high renown,
Out searching for a singing-bird
Whose voice, the sweetest ever heard,
Shall cheer me in my hours of gloom,
And coax my dead loves back to bloom."

"Take me, O king," the gray bird said.
"A sad and lonely life I 've led,
Singing with not a soul to hear,
Pining for but one word of cheer."

"Thou!" cried the king, half in surprise,
A sudden anger in his eyes —
"Thou insignificant, nameless bird!
Thou ninny, hast thou never heard
Of my grand palace and my throne
Of pearl and gold and precious stone?
Thou gray, sad eyed, presumptuous thing!
Thou entertain a court and king!
Begone! Say not another word:
My cage must hold a royal bird."

There came a silken sound of wings
Above the brooklet's murmurings;
The wind fell still upon the grass
To watch the gray bird upward pass;
The sunlight milder, softer grew;
The leaves took on a tenderer hue —
As if all Nature, gently stirred,
Bade farewell to the going bird.

The monarch stood with lips compressed,
Regret and choler in his breast,
While from the sky, well-sent and strong,
Came back a Parthian shaft of song.

THE GOLD–BIRD.

THE gold-bird came in the May morn
  Down fragrant billows of southwest weather:
He fell, like a flame, in the sweet thorn, —
  He and his brown mate close together.

This was the promise of May-time;
  Wind-song and bird-song sweetly flowing
Over the thorn, like a love-rhyme,
  Where buds were breaking and flowers were
      blowing.

The gold-bird sang to his brown mate
  A song no words of mine may render,
While she built a nest in the sweet thorn,
  In the dusky deeps of the thorn leaves
      tender.

This was the joy of the May-time:
  A bird like a flame and a love like fire,

The weather set to a soft tune
  Thrilled and filled with pure desire.

The gold-bird sat by his brown mate,
  Brooding their young through the drowsy weather,
And when June came with its red heat
  The birds and their brood flew off together.

O sweet fulfillment of May-time!
  A gold-bird, a brown mate, a nest and fruition
Of all the joys of a love-song!
  This was the whole of the gold-bird's mission.

THE KINGFISHER.

HE laughs by the summer stream
Where the lilies nod and dream,
As through the sheen of water cool and clear
He sees the chub and sunfish cutting sheer.

His are resplendent eyes ;
His mien is kingliwise ;
And down the May wind rides he like a king,
With more than royal purple on his wing.

His palace is the brake
Where the rushes shine and shake ;
His music is the murmur of the stream,
And that leaf-rustle where the lilies dream.

Such life as his would be
A more than heaven to me :
All sun, all bloom, all happy weather,
All joys bound in a sheaf together.

No wonder he laughs so loud!
No wonder he looks so proud!
There are great kings would give their royalty
To have one day of his felicity!

UNAWARE.

THERE is a song some one must sing,
  In tender tones and low,
With pink lips curled and quivering,
  And eyes with dreams aglow.

There is some one must hear the tune,
  And feel the thrilling words,
As flowers feel, in early June,
  The wings of humming-birds.

And she who sings must never learn
  What good her song has done,
Albeit the hearer slowly turn
  Him drowsily, as one

Who feels through all his being thrown
  The influence sweet and slight
Of strange, elusive perfume, blown
  Off dewy groves by night!

FAREWELL.

FAREWELL! It is no sorrowful word.
  It has never had a pang for me.
Sweet as the last song of a bird,
  Soft as a wind-swell from the sea,
            The word Farewell.

I part with you as oft before
  I 've parted with dear friends and sweet,
And now I shake (forevermore)
  Your memory's gold-dust from my feet.
            Farewell! farewell!

Soon I shall find a new sweet face,
  And other eyes as pure and strong
As yours are now, and then a space
  Of life that ripples into song,
            And then farewell!

Farewell ! farewell ! Throw me a kiss !
  How fast the distance grows between !
Now memory fades — a film of bliss,
  A far-off mist of silvery sheen :
        Good-by ! farewell !

www.ingramcontent.com/pod-product-compliance
Lightning Source LLC
LaVergne TN
LVHW011202110826
845150LV00006B/1298

* 9 7 8 1 4 2 5 5 1 8 6 5 3 *